Charlie Sanders's
TALES FROM THE DETROIT LIONS

Charlie Sanders

with Larry Paladino

www.SportsPublishingLLC.com

ISBN: 1-58261-910-7

© 2005 by Charlie Sanders and Larry Paladino

All rights reserved. Except for use in a review, the reproduction or utilization of this work in any form or by any electronic, mechanical, or other means, now known or hereafter invented, including xerography, photocopying, and recording, and in any information storage and retrieval system, is forbidden without the written permission of the publisher.

Publishers: Peter L. Bannon and Joseph J. Bannon Sr.
Senior managing editor: Susan M. Moyer
Acquisitions editor: Mike Pearson
Developmental editor: Regina D. Sabbia
Art director: K. Jeffrey Higgerson
Dust jacket design: Dustin J. Hubbart
Project manager: Kathryn R. Holleman
Imaging: Dustin J. Hubbart and Kathryn R. Holleman
Photo editor: Erin Linden-Levy
Vice president of sales and marketing: Kevin King
Media and promotions managers: Jonathan Patterson (regional),
    Randy Fouts (national), Maurey Williamson (print)

Printed in the United States of America

Sports Publishing L.L.C.
804 North Neil Street
Champaign, IL 61820

Phone: 1-877-424-2665
Fax: 217-363-2073
www.SportsPublishingLLC.com

After much thought, I've chosen to dedicate this book to my mother, Parteacher. She passed away at age 28 when I was only two years old. Though I never really knew her, I feel that she is the angel who has guided, encouraged, and protected me. The changes that my dad, Nathan, made in our lives as a result of mom's passing ultimately created changes and opportunities that
I may not have had otherwise.
Sometimes in loss and adversity we find a silver lining if we look for one. I know that mine came to me in the silver and Honolulu blue colors of the Detroit Lions. I am happy to have worn those colors and pleased to have been part of an organization and a larger community that has
always felt like family to me.
Thanks, Mom!

—C.S.

To Marilyn, Sheri, Lisa, Anthony, Dominic, Natalie, and Christian. May they understand that the world of long ago wasn't really much different from today. Look to the future with vision, but with a respect for those whose accomplishments—and failures—forged the way before them.

—L.P.

CONTENTS

Foreword by Greg Landry vii
Foreword by Lem Barney viii
Preface ix
Acknowledgments xi
Introduction xii

Chapter 1: Anecdote Magnets 1

Chapter 2: Barnstormers 15

Chapter 3: Baseball Beckoned 17

Chapter 4: Basketball Gridders 21

Chapter 5: 'Big Bucks' 24

Chapter 6: Breaking Barriers 25

Chapter 7: Coach Carousel 27

Chapter 8: Conniving and Conspiracy 40

Chapter 9: Cup of Coffee 44

Chapter 10: Draft/Free Agent Debacles, Successes ... 47

Chapter 11: Eclectic Execs 50

Chapter 12: Embarrassing Moments 53

Chapter 13: Fashion Plates? 56

Chapter 14: Fifth Estate 58

Chapter 15: Frustrating Rivalry 62

Chapter 16: Gifted Players 63

Chapter 17: Injury Setbacks and Medical Oddities 72

Chapter 18: Innovators and Innovations 76

Chapter 19: Knuckle Sandwiches 83

Chapter 20: Long Arm of the Law 90

Chapter 21: Mascot Minutiae 93

Chapter 22: Milestone Moments 96

Chapter 23: Military Commitments 97

Chapter 24: Musical Inclinations 104

Chapter 25: Nicknames 107

Chapter 26: Ornery Opponents 108

Chapter 27: Outside the Lines 111

Chapter 28: Owners' Travails 117

Chapter 29: 'Paper Lion' 120

Chapter 30: Paying the Bills 124

Chapter 31: Politics 126

Chapter 32: Practical Jokes 130

Chapter 33: Publicity: Stunts and More 136

Chapter 34: Quarterback Tales 140

Chapter 35: Rival Leagues 143

Chapter 36: Stadium Stories 147

Chapter 37: Students of the Game 151

Chapter 38: Teaser Season 153

Chapter 39: Terrific Toes 155

Chapter 40: Then and Now 158

Chapter 41: Tough Guys 163

Chapter 42: Trainer Tips 165

Chapter 43: Tragedies 166

Chapter 44: Travel Travails 171

Chapter 45: TV Tales 173

Chapter 46: Weather Adventures 176

FOREWORD

BY GREG LANDRY

No one drafted by National Football League teams could really know what to expect. We have our college experience and our goals if we turn pro, but who can really say what will happen after we get selected?

Well, I was fortunate in that Detroit drafted me in the first round in 1968, and eventually I became the starting quarterback and had a successful 11-year career with the Lions.

How was I to know, though, that in that same draft, in the third round, would be a guy named Charlie Sanders who would go on to become perhaps the finest tight end in the history of the Lions. What quarterback wouldn't want a tight end like him, a big guy who was fast, had great hands, and could block like any top lineman?

Our careers with Detroit ran parallel, and he's been a friend all these years. So it was with great interest that I heard he was writing a book of Lions stories. He certainly is a good person to do it, having been involved with the team in one capacity or another almost steadily since we both reported to training camp at Cranbrook School back in 1968.

A lot of things go on behind the scenes, in training camp, on the sidelines, after games, and at practice, and it would all be confined to our memories unless someone like Charlie got around to recording those stories for posterity, as he has done in this book.

Lions history goes back to the early 1930s, though, and Charlie and co-writer Larry Paladino have come up with many tales from eras gone by. We are fortunate to have the opportunity to relive those old stories. They should provide plenty of conversation for Lions fans and all football buffs everywhere.

Greg Landry, Detroit's top draft pick in 1968 from Massachusetts, had a standout 11-year career with the Lions.
Photo courtesy of the Detroit Lions

FOREWORD

BY LEM BARNEY

When I heard my friend Charlie "Satch" Sanders was writing a book of Detroit Lions stories it made me feel good—until I thought to myself, "Oh, I wonder if he's going to tell them about that time when…"

Seriously, there were lots of things that went on, both off and on the field, that would make great reading. Some probably were forgotten long ago, only to be rekindled at Lions' alumni functions when the guys get together and start reminiscing. It's kind of like when veterans groups, or college or high school classmates, get together for reunions. The stories come from different perspectives and may not be told the same as years go by. But any telling of these tales seems worthwhile, regardless of the twists in the narrations, and I admire Charlie for his efforts in seeing that this material doesn't get lost forever.

What a great guy Charlie was to have as a teammate and roommate. We played on different sides of the ball, and I got a kick out of playing cornerback in practice sometimes when he'd try to play from a wide-out position and try to beat me on a pass route. I used to josh with him about that. It was such a privilege that our careers nearly coincided. What a great tight end he was, and now I'll be able to know him as an author, as well.

This book isn't going to just appeal to Lions fans, though, because many of the stories contain human drama or foibles that will be universally recognized. And it is good for me, as a former player, to be able to read about the things that happened to many of those who came before me and realize things never really change much over the decades.

Charlie Sanders (84) and Lem Barney (20) flank ex-Lion assistant coach Chuck Knox of the Rams at the 1977 Pro Bowl game.
Photo courtesy of the Detroit Lions

I'm sure you will enjoy these Lions tales, just as I'm sure Charlie has enjoyed resurrecting them.

PREFACE

Athletes and anecdotes pretty much go hand in hand. Anyone who has followed any professional sport probably has heard many tales of their favorite players or stories of those from eras gone by.

Indeed, some of the better anecdotes can be gleaned from the "old days," when people got their fix of mostly off-the-field sports stories from newspapers.

That was long before the arrival of infinitesimal television stations through cable and satellite and the need to fill those airways with something, anything, just to fill time and sell ads. Every morsel of an athlete's life nowadays goes under the broadcast microscope, it seems: dirty laundry, personal foibles, or any human faux pas.

It's almost a wonder that there's an actual sport at play considering the way the radio and TV sports talk shows, and even game color commentators, rant about the latest misstep of a star athlete, or that of someone not remotely a star but with a penchant for getting into trouble.

If there's an off-the-wall happening from the last decade, you probably heard about it ad nauseam. That's why in *Charlie Sanders's Tales from the Detroit Lions* we have endeavored to bring you mostly long-forgotten stories from another era. There is a lot here from the franchise's early days and its championship years of the 1950s and also through the 1970s. Interspersed are some more recent tidbits from the 1980s, 1990s, and beyond.

Sanders, probably the greatest Lions tight end of all time, has collaborated with long-time sports writer Larry Paladino to compile this array of anecdotes that are often humorous, sometimes poignant, or just plain insightful. Many items likely were the talk of the town for a while, back in the days when most people actually got their news from newspapers (and reporters might even be found tipping a few at the end of the bar with the players from time to time). But these tales might fade into history if not for this effort.

We'll start off with "Anecdote Magnets"—several players who seemed automatically to generate interesting stories: Les Bingaman, Alex Karras, Bobby Layne, and Joe Don Looney. But there were others whose tales should be told, like a couple World War II heroes who used to play with the Lions, Maurice Britt and Charles Tripson, and other ex-Lions who died in the service of their country. The war interrupted the chance for them to make a mark on the gridiron, but they certainly made one on the battlefields—and who among Lions fans even knows of them or their deeds? Britt won the Medal of Honor and Tripson the Navy Cross.

Sometimes it was difficult to categorize tales, so some chapters might have two-dozen items and others just one. We've got a chapter simply listing nicknames. Another highlights off-the-field activities. And of course there had to be chapters on practical jokes and embarrassing moments.

A chapter on "Innovators and Innovations" provides a glimpse at some things Lions pioneered. There certainly is a practical jokes chapter, plus one on embarrassing moments. Before they were pros, Lions achieved greatness in college in football or other sports and many of those are outlined in a "Pre-Pro Heroes" chapter. Publicity stunts get their due, as do some tragedies, rival league incursions, barroom brawls, and so much more.

In the 70-plus years of Lions history the team has seen roughly 1,200 players wear the Honolulu Blue and Silver, not counting the many more who were drafted or signed and were Lions only in training camps. There have been more than 175 coaches, including 20 head coaches, for the franchise, plus countless executives and other staff personnel.

Needless to say, there is the potential of at least one interesting story on each one of them, but such a book would take volumes. So we've gleaned what we feel are a representative array of interesting tidbits to make you smile or tweak your intellect and possibly provide anecdote fodder for the next time you're playing cards with your friends or at somebody's house watching football together.

Sanders wrote some of the tales in first person because he experienced them himself or was on the team or with the organization at the time. The others have been taken mostly from the Lions' huge newspaper clip files or from Paladino's personal files from some 35 years of covering sports for the Associated Press, newspapers and magazines.

But Sanders often has connections one way or another with even some of the older tales, through alumni functions, personal research, and just plain recollections from so many years with the Lions.

ACKNOWLEDGMENTS

A great deal of thanks to all my teammates for providing me with such great memories, some of which are shared in this book. I would like to thank the greatest fans in the NFL, Detroit Lions fans, for the love and fantastic support they showed me as a player. Thanks for making life for my family and me a memorable one.

I'd also like to thank the Detroit Lions organization and the owner, Mr. William Clay Ford, for all he and his family have provided for my family and me. I personally can say he is the best owner in the NFL. It has been a pleasure to have known and been employed by him for over 35 years. Hopefully we have developed the respect for one another and what we both desire for the organization and its fans.

There aren't enough thanks for the writer, Larry Paladino, and all the time he devoted to this book. The quality of work and the dedication he showed was outstanding. I must say that without him there would be nothing to read.

To the PR department of the Detroit Lions, I give thanks for your support. Without the help of Dee Caldwell and Matt Barnhart, this book would not be complete. Additionally, thanks go to Sports Publishing L.L.C. of Champaign, Illinois, and its fine staff, including Gina Sabbia who coordinated this project, and Mike Pearson who first approached me with the concept, and Jonathan Patterson who will help us get this book into the hands of Lion fans everywhere.

—CHARLIE SANDERS

INTRODUCTION

Charlie Sanders has been part of the Lions all but a few years of his adult life since coming to Detroit from the University of Minnesota in the 1968 draft. He went on to have perhaps the greatest career for a tight end in Lions history.

He has served the organization in a number of capacities since his playing days ended after the 1977 season, the latest as assistant director of pro personnel. Blend his fine Big Ten education with his on-the-field accomplishments and his executive positions, and you have an articulate human reservoir of first-hand involvement in the team for all or parts of five decades.

So it would seem he is a natural to use those skills to author this book of Lions anecdotes, along with Larry Paladino, who has been writing sports in Detroit since the year Sanders was drafted. Together they have compiled this array of tales, most long forgotten but resurrected from the yellowing newspaper pages of Lions scrapbooks that go back to the early 1930s.

Though Sanders calls the Detroit area his home, he hails from North Carolina and still has relatives there. Before getting into the book, he briefly discussed some of his background.

"Dad raised hogs on our farm and enlisted in the Army after my mother's death," he said. "After his release from the military he obtained his master's degree in engineering.

"I grew up on a farm and never touched a football in terms of organized sports until the 10th grade. You just didn't have time for sports. You had to do your chores....When dad got a job at North Carolina A&T in Greensboro we moved there."

Sanders's introduction to organized sports came in the ninth grade when he played basketball. "I had a pretty good basketball career in high school," he said. "Our coach from junior high was being transferred to the senior high school and asked me if I could play. I said yeah, but he said I wasn't good enough. I took it as a challenge." He ended up excelling not just in basketball, but also in football and baseball.

"I actually went to the University of Minnesota to play football and basketball," Sanders said. "In basketball, I only played center in high school. When I went out for the freshman team at Minnesota, all of a sudden this guy walks out and he's about seven-feet tall. I said this isn't for me, and I concentrated on football."

The Golden Gophers recruited him as a wide receiver, so that's what he started out as. The next year they moved him to safety, and a year later after defensive end Aaron Brown got drafted by the NFL, Sanders was moved to that position. He

Basketball was Charlie Sanders's first sports love. Here he shoots a lay-up for the Lions team in a charity game in 1975 against the Police Athletic League team in Pontiac.
Photo courtesy of the Detroit Lions

didn't play tight end until his senior year. "I enjoyed it but didn't envision these things that have happened," he said.

He had a chance to go to Wake Forest in North Carolina as the first black athlete there. In fact, he said, it was Brian Piccolo, the player made famous by the movie *Brian's Song*, who took him out on his recruiting visit. His second trip was to Minnesota, and he decided to go there partly because he had a friend there, Lou Hudson, a basketball teammate from high school (and who eventually went on to play with the Los Angeles Lakers).

"I grew up in the South and you wondered if there was another world out there," he said. "My father taught [civil rights leader] Jesse Jackson and gave him a few Fs on his engineering papers."

In Minneapolis, Sanders went into an ice cream parlor and "that was the first time I went in a front door without hearing necks cracking from white people turning their heads to look at you and leave you with the impression they'd never seen black people before. To me, I knew something was different. That was the major reason I decided to go to Minnesota. I wanted to get as far away from the South as I could."

"In the South I was shot at," he said. "I was called a nigger by a two-year-old in a restaurant, and her mother, who I'm sure she learned it from, slapped her. We've been shot at trick-or-treating in our own neighborhood. It was important that I get out of that environment. If I stayed I think I would have looked at people in a totally different way."

Minnesota had already gotten some top black players from the South, like Bobby Bell and Carl Eller, plus Sandy Stephens from Pennsylvania. But out of a student population of about 50,000, about 20 were black and "you knew they were all athletes," Sanders said.

Murray Warmath was Sanders's coach in college and "I really learned to understand the game of football under him."

Sanders's father, who died in 1982, never pushed him into sports, Charlie said, and instead "he wanted me to do everything but play sports because he felt you had your work and you had your studies. Then you had your sports. I can understand it now. Being an educator, a professor, at that time, he didn't know what sports could bring to black athletes, so he felt education came first. He was the kind who believed you had to earn the right. I don't think he ever saw me play but one game live, that was a Lions game on Thanksgiving."

Sanders never pushed any of his nine children into sports, going with the philosophy that if they liked it they could do it. "I've been fortunate that they've all gotten into something they enjoy," he said. "That's what it's all about. You don't get a lot out of anything when you're forced into doing something."

He won 10 game balls in his Lions career, and that was good, he said, since, "I had to get at least nine because I had to get one for each of my kids."

Sanders was inducted into the Michigan Sports Hall of Fame in 1990 and into the North Carolina Sports Hall of Fame in 1997. He also is in the Dudley (North Carolina) High School Hall of Fame and is a nominee for the NFL Hall of Fame and almost assuredly will wind up in the University of Minnesota Hall of Fame. The nine children of he and his wife, Georgianna, are: Mia, Charese, Mary Jo, Georgianna, Charlie Jr., Nathalie, Tallisa, Wayne, and Jordan.

—LARRY PALADINO

1

ANECDOTE MAGNETS

While there are countless anecdotes involving the Detroit Lions (some probably long ago lost to history), a handful of players seemed to be anecdote magnets. Among them were Les Bingaman, Alex Karras, Bobby Layne, and Joe Don Looney. I was a teammate of Karras, and I met and spoke with Layne at a banquet. There also are parallels to some of the Bingaman and Looney tales over my nearly 40 years with the Lions organization. Following are a few of the stories, some familiar and some not so familiar.

Freight Weight

Those who remember Lester Alonzo 'Bingo' Bingaman (G, 1948-1954; assistant coach, 1961-1964) during his days on the great Lions teams of the early 1950s remember a huge man, one of the heaviest in the NFL at about 350 pounds in days when the biggest players were maybe 250. We had at least one enormous player like that, tackle Roger Brown. I think only the trainer and coach knew how much he weighed. He was one of the renowned "Fearsome Foursome" front defensive line of the Lions and was a player when Bingaman was an assistant coach for Detroit.

In a roundabout way, when the Lions traded Brown to the Los Angeles Rams after the 1966 season, it helped make me a Lion. When the team drafted me on the third round in 1968, it got the selection in a trade from Cleveland through Los Angeles, stemming from the Brown trade. The Lions got quarterback Bill Munson from the Rams in that deal.

Brown and Bingaman were so heavy they couldn't be weighed on the regular team scale that just went up to 300 pounds. When Bingaman was at his peak weight, coaches argued about how much he weighed and finally decided to settle arguments by taking him to a freight depot to weigh him. He tipped the truck scales at 349 1/2 pounds. Coach Buddy Parker had guessed Bingaman was close to 400 pounds "and that hurt Bingo's feelings," quarterback Bobby Layne told a magazine writer. To

Les Bingaman wasn't huge, about five foot 11, 250 pounds, when he joined the Lions in 1948, but eventually in the mid-1950s he was 6-2, 349 1/2—a weight determined from a truck depot scale. *Photo courtesy of the Detroit Lions*

determine Brown's weight, they took him to a meat market to use a scale designed for huge carcasses.

Brown was big from the beginning, but a look at the press guides over the years shows how Bingaman changed dramatically in a few years. The 1949 guide listed the star from Illinois at five foot 11, 250 pounds. By 1952, he was 6-3, 280. The following year, for some reason, he was back down to 6-2, but up in weight to 295. Then, in 1954, his final season as a Lions player, he was listed at 6-3, but with a weight that had ballooned to 335, but later determined to be 349 1/2.

Bingaman's father, who was six foot four, 230 pounds, died when Les was five. At Lew Wallace High School in Gary, Indiana, Les was so agile he was a guard on the basketball team. He became perhaps the most famous middle guard in pro football history in the 1950s as a main cog in a five-man defensive line that helped propel the Lions to three Western Conference championships and two NFL titles through 1954. He was their No. 3 draft pick after playing on Illinois's 1947 Rose Bowl championship team.

He went into the bar business after his Lions career, but sold his bar in 1960 to come back to Detroit as an assistant coach. He was an assistant with the Miami Dolphins from 1966 until his death November 20, 1970. He was elected to the Michigan Sports Hall of Fame the next year.

AIRCRAFT CHALLENGES

I never was fond of flying, but at least in my era the planes were a bit more substantial than they were a couple decades earlier when heavy loads were much more of a concern. There never was a time when we had to kick anyone off the plane because they were too heavy, but that's what happened once with Bingaman.

A feature in the October 29, 1954, issue of *Collier's* magazine called him "Pro football's immovable object." The story, by Bill Fay, said he was the biggest man in the game and "when blockers charge him, he just stomachs 'em aside....There's no need for a linebacker behind Bingo." Also, Fay said, Bingaman "is fast on his feet—for about nine yards."

The article was replete with "Bingo" anecdotes, like the time in 1953 when the Lions were boarding a DC-6 flight to San Francisco. The pilot watched Bingaman trudging up the loading ramp and said to the stewardess, "I said it to Orville and I said it to Wilbur, and I'll say it again: This thing will never get off the ground."

Only once, though, was he denied passage. That was in 1952 when the Lions were returning from Little Rock, Arkansas, after an exhibition game. The pilot said he was able to take off on the trip from Detroit's Willow Run Airport because the runway was long enough, but the Little Rock runway was 300 feet shorter "and that big guy could make an awful difference in the takeoff." So he and 260-pound Leon Hart got off the plane to lighten the load by some 600 pounds and they had to charter a plane to get back to Detroit.

Elevator Blues

I've gotten on plenty of elevators with huge teammates and never had any qualms about it, until I spotted a magazine article in our archives. There was a time in Birmingham, Alabama, when, according to the 1954 *Collier's* article, Bingaman stepped into the hotel elevator with four other players—Cloyce Box, Thurman McGraw, Lou Creekmur, and Pat Harder—and said, "Six please." The elevator rose to the second floor and then there was a loud metallic clank as though a cable had snapped. The car plummeted to the basement. Nobody was hurt and Bingaman denied responsibility, but Bill Fay reported, "None of the Lions would ride in an elevator with him after that."

'Jackie Gleason in Spiked Shoes'

My old teammate Alex Karras (DT, 1958-1962; 1963-1970) was a Detroit Lions superstar long before his mug became a familiar sight in movies and on television. By 1962 the press was getting to know him pretty well as the season wound down, the *Free Press*'s George Puscas wrote a color feature on him.

"He breaks 'em up in the locker room. He keeps 'em loose on the practice field. He is beyond being one of the best defensive tackles in football, he's one of the best mimics of his game, a sort of Jackie Gleason in spiked shoes," he wrote. "There's a strange paradox in Karras. For although he is the funniest Lion, he is also the angriest."

It was barely a month later, though, in January 1963, that Karras treatened to quit the team if it tried to force him to get rid of his part ownership in the Lindell Athletic Club bar downtown. It was during this time the NFL was investigating gambling in the league (and gamblers frequented the Lindell).

On April 17 the NFL indefinitely banished Karras for gambling on football and fined Joe Schmidt, Wayne Walker, Gary Lowe, John Gordy, and Sam Williams $2,000 each. Paul Hornung of Green Bay also was suspended. The Lions fines were for betting on the 1962 championship game between Green Bay and the New York Giants.

Two Bruisers Brawl

Less than a week after Karras's suspension, he got into his infamous brawl with pro wrestler Dick the Bruiser at 1 a.m. in the Lindell, the well-known sports bar that still was one of the spots to go to when I joined the team. Co-owner Jimmy Butsicaris was involved in the brawl, as well as five bar patrons, when the police came in. It took eight officers to wrestle the 250-pound Bruiser (34-year-old Richard Afflis) to the floor and handcuff him behind his back. He suffered a cut above the left eye that took five stitches at Receiving Hospital to close.

Alex Karras was a locker-room funny man, but he had his angry side.
Photo courtesy of the Detroit Lions

Butsicaris later filed an aggravated assault complaint against Afflis, who he said came into the bar and used abusive language to him and Karras after Butsicaris refused to serve him. Afflis grabbed him by the shirt and swung at him, according to the report. Bruiser's cut came from a pool cue.

The News' story on the incident quoted Afflis as saying Karras had called him a "third-rate football player" from the days Afflis played with the Packers (1951-54), and he added, "I had nothing against Karras until I heard what he was saying about me." Karras denied he made the "third-rate" comment. The police commissioner recommended the Lindell move from Bagley and Cass to Cass and Michigan. It's anyone's guess what difference that would make.

HYPE FOR COBO MATCH?

Karras had baby bird legs and a big upper body, but good lateral movement. He probably was more bark than bite. It was amazing to me that he ended up fighting someone like Dick the Bruiser, but I think it was more to defend his reputation than anything else.

Perhaps the Lindell brawl was just something to bolster interest in the wrestling match the former college wrestler Karras would have with The Bruiser at Cobo Arena. The match was triggered by the Bruiser's heckling of Karras over the fight he got into during a charity basketball game, the same kind of game I often played in a few years later.

"He loves to wrestle skinny-necked wrestlers because he knows he can't lose," the wrestler said in an April 14 *Free Press* story. "That's the reason he quit wrestling. He knew sooner or later he'd have to meet me, and the thought of it scared him." A crowd estimated between 6,500 and 10,000 showed up at Cobo Arena and saw Karras last just 11 minutes and 21 seconds against The Bruiser.

Karras wasn't playing football, but he was still a publicity lightning rod and in the summer, *Look* magazine's Tim Cohane wrote a feature on pro football centered on Karras. In mid-November, NFL Commissioner Pete Rozelle said Karras had to cut all ties with the Lindell or he couldn't return to play in 1964. Ten days later Karras agreed.

ONLY BRO COMBO

When the Lions acquired guard Ted Karras, an ex-Marine, from the Washington Redskins, in 1965, that put him on a team with his brother, Alex, making them the only brother combination in the NFL.

Practically Blind

Alex Karras wore Coke bottle-sized lenses in his glasses off the field. On the field he'd just tackle any blur he saw coming through the line, whether or not it might happen to be one of his teammates. It might have been that sight problem that helped make him the great athlete he was, because it forced him to play by instinct.

Football First Love

One key thing about Karras was you never knew exactly what he felt because he had the ability to hide his acting skill—and that made him a good actor. It was hard for me to get a read on him. He lived off that reputation. I never personally saw him get angry and beat up anybody.

When the Lions cut Karras in September 1971, he was bitter because he wanted to play one more year before pursuing an acting career. "I cannot believe that the Lions' decision to place me on waivers is based on a fair assessment of my performance on the field. There are other factors involved," he said at a news conference he held at a friend's auto dealership in the suburb of Oak Park.

It was the second scratch from a Detroit sports roster of a heralded star in less than a week. Six days earlier, hockey's Gordie Howe of the Red Wings announced his retirement after 25 years as a Red Wing.

"I came back to the Detroit Lions this season for just one reason," Karras said in his formal written statement. "I felt the Lions had a chance to go all the way, and I sincerely believe I could contribute something of value to the club. I had planned to retire and pursue my other interests and had been in negotiations for various movie and television roles. My manager, Tom Vance, and I had actually suspended negotiations for a television series and one definite movie role because of my decision to give one more year, at least, to my first love, football."

Coach Joe Schmidt said it was his decision alone to let Karras go and called him "the greatest defensive lineman the Lions ever had."

Karras had become somewhat of a thorn in the side of Lions management ever since his return from his suspension in 1964. As always, he was very quotable, and his casual humor got him numerous TV appearances and mentions in magazines and newspapers, sometimes being critical of Rozelle or Lions owner William Clay Ford.

"Perhaps there is no room in the world of sports these days for an athlete who has an opinion on anything except his own sport," Karras said, in the cramped dealership conference room.

"I have a wife, and children, and I pay my bills like everyone else. Therefore, I think I am entitled to the same considerations as other human beings, and that includes having the right to express myself on something other than playing defensive tackle."

Karras had been one of the most prominent active Lions players featured in the movie *Paper Lion*, about writer George Plimpton's first-hand tryout with the team at training camp in Florida in 1963. Soon after his departure from football, Karras was a busy actor, and his career really took off with his role in the Mel Brooks movie comedy *Blazing Saddles*. He also was the star of the successful TV situation comedy *Webster* and the classic TV miniseries *Centennial*.

HE AIN'T DRUNK

Bobby Layne (1950-1958), the Lions' NFL Hall of Fame quarterback from their championship years of the 1950s, was noted for drinking and bar hopping. I thought that was all just talk until I sat down with him at a sports banquet in Flint, Michigan. I jokingly asked him to defend some of the stories about him and his drinking. Laughingly, he told me he couldn't remember a day that he hadn't been drinking—and I believe he was telling the honest-to-God's truth.

As a matter of fact, he said the day that he died he wanted people at his funeral to drink and have fun, because that's the way he looked at life. It was all fun to him. So I guess alcohol was a big part of his life and he was able to function.

He once fought a traffic ticket in court and beat a drunk driving charge when his lawyer convinced the jury that the arresting officer mistook his Texas drawl for a drunken slur. Afterwards, the Lions held a "not-guilty" party, and equipment manager Friday Macklem hung a banner that read: "Ah all ain't drunk, ah'm from Texas." Once commenting on the drug and other legal problems of some of today's pros, Layne said: "The worst thing any of us did was drink beer."

There were many who believed he played better when he had been out on a binge. He had probably the highest salary on the team and was generous with his money. "I didn't try to pick up every tab, but I picked up my share," he said. The story on him was that he became very successful in the oil business. In the era he played, it wasn't the greatest life for many after their football careers were over, because there wasn't player insurance and not much income. Bobby Layne was a guy who took care of the old-timers, the guys on his team who had hard times. He had a very generous heart and a lot of guys looked up to him not only for leadership, but also for financial advice and assistance.

KIDS MISS CURFEW

Normally, Layne's coach, Buddy Parker, didn't impose a curfew during training camp. But when the Lions were in Chicago to play the College All-Stars he set an 11 p.m. deadline for players to be in their hotel rooms and in bed. He figured Layne would have his teammates out partying.

Sure enough, at 11 p.m. the coach went down the hall and checked on all the veterans' rooms and nearly all were empty at 11. Not even his son, Bobby, and Layne's eight-year-old son, Rob, who were rooming together, were there and

Quarterback Bobby Layne had a reputation for partying, but his field leadership and talent guided the Lions in their championship heyday of the 1950s and put him into the NFL Hall of Fame. *Photo courtesy of the Detroit Lions*

someone heard Parker shout out, "My God, even the kids aren't in yet!" It turned out that end Sonny Gandee had taken them to a drive-in movie but fell asleep in the car.

Parker gave the recalcitrant players the choice of paying a $100 fine or going through an extra tough workout. Layne could afford the fine better than the others, but he said he'd take the practice punishment, and everyone went along. The toughest drill was pushing the blocking sled the length of the field five times and back. Players got sick, but Layne seemed OK, and Parker said since he was doing so well maybe they should do it again. That prompted Layne to yell, "Fall out!" whereupon everyone dispersed.

Layne related the story in 1982 when we hosted Super Bowl XVI at the Silverdome. He did the official toss of the coin. Layne said Harley Sewell was one of the Lions who didn't miss curfew, yet he went through the punishment workout with everyone else. He said that Parker asked him why and Sewell just said he "didn't want to miss anything."

Not Faster, Just Lighter

Layne was one of the last pros who didn't wear a face mask. "I tried every year to wear one," he said. "I couldn't get used to it. It bothered my vision. I would have worn it if I could." He wore only small shoulder pads. He didn't wear thigh, hip, or kneepads. It didn't make him feel faster, he said, "but it made me feel lighter."

Six-Play Team

In 1968, Layne and ex-teammates Sewell and Doak Walker coached the Texas high school all-star team to a victory over a team of Pennsylvania all-stars for the fourth consecutive year. His emphasis was on keeping things simple.

"Coaches are too complex," he said. "I firmly believe you should take blackboards away from coaches. You're better off keeping it simple. One year we gave our kids six running plays, then Doak came up with another. Harley said, 'Coach, don't you think we're maybe over-coaching 'em?' I said, 'Yeah, darned right.' So we dropped it and stuck with just six plays, and the kids went out and did great."

Ignored the Coach

A *Newsweek* magazine article from the mid-1950s said the reason Parker didn't send in plays for Layne was, "If I sent in plays he wouldn't pay any attention. He's a take-charge guy."

Walker once said Layne "never lost a game in his life, time just ran out on him." Another ex-teammate, Yale Lary said, "When Bobby said block, you blocked."

Harley Sewell didn't have to join his teammates in a grueling practice punishment for missing curfew before the All-Star game one year, but he did it anyway because he didn't want to be left out. *Photo courtesy of the Detroit Lions*

Among the other telling quotes about Layne was this from bombastic sportscaster Howard Cosell: "There was Waterfield. And Graham. And Van Brocklin. And Unitas. Now some say Starr. Others say Tittle, but he never won the big one. But for those of us who know the game, there was only one quarterback—Bobby Layne."

Sports writer Mickey Herskowitz said of Layne: "There never was a bigger blue-collar hero in the whole blessed sport than Bobby Layne."

BOBBY WHO? ARTHUR WHO?

Just about everyone in the 1950s, Detroit or elsewhere, knew who Bobby Layne was. He had quarterbacked the team to a couple NFL championships. But in September 1955 at a party at the home of General Motors executive Harold Boyer, TV and radio star Arthur Godfrey was introduced to Layne and asked him (according to Free Press "Town Crier" Mark Beltaire), "What do you do for a living?" Layne responded, "Oh, I play a little football. What do you do?" Godfrey burst out laughing and the two wound up becoming best of friends.

LOONEY TUNES

I joined the Lions shortly after the brief career of Joe Don Looney with the team, subsequently the stories I heard about him were pretty fresh. His personality certainly mirrored his name. Because of his free spirit, he passed through four colleges and five NFL teams in eight years. The New York Giants drafted the Oklahoma halfback in the first round in 1964, but he didn't survive training camp.

When he refused to talk to the New York press, an executive intervened, but Looney said he still wouldn't talk. A note was slipped under his door saying he was assessed a $50 fine for his refusal. Looney tore it up and gave it to the staff member—under HIS door, wrote Ben Dunn of *The News*. He said twice Looney was told by Giants coaches that when hitting the blocking dummy he should "hit it and move." He was knocked down by the sled twice, got angry, and tore the blocking dummy off its support and wrestled it to the ground, cursing, screaming, and kicking.

'CRAZIER THAN ME'

Detroit must have figured it could handle Looney because it acquired him from Baltimore in 1965 for linebacker Dennis Gaubatz. He lasted two seasons. Alex Hawkins, a teammate with him at Baltimore, said he was asked by coach Don Shula one year to be Looney's roommate. "I told Shula that I couldn't go to sleep in the same room with anyone crazier than me." Sonny Eliot, funnyman weatherman for eons in Detroit, said Looney once said to him: "I never met a man I didn't like—except Will Rogers."

Had a Few Beers

In another tale written by Ben Dunn, Looney broke down the door of a neighbor's apartment in Baltimore and struck a friend of the neighbor. In court he was fined $150 and put on a year's probation. "It was all a big mistake," Looney said. "I went off the deep end. I had a few beers.

"I feel I know what this pro game is all about now. It takes a little while to get acclimated. I'll be all right if I can play regularly."

Bad Advice?

When Joe Schmidt was an assistant coach with Detroit he tried to give the undisciplined Looney some advice: "You've got to work hard in this league. I've been with the club for 12 years and I've never missed a practice." Responded Looney: "Joe, you should take a day off once in a while." He promptly was suspended.

There was another time when Schmidt wanted to send him into a game in which the Lions were losing by a lot. Looney looked at the scoreboard and said he wasn't going in because there was no chance to win. And still another time, under similar conditions, he asked Schmidt if he wanted him to go in to win it or just tie it.

'Like a Slave'

Shortly after the start of 1965 training camp, Looney got into a scuffle at a pancake house in Royal Oak, then in early September he missed a practice and the *Free Press* headline read: 'Back in the Doghouse Again'. Less than two weeks later he was involved in another incident, a shouting match at a bar.

Looney wasn't mellower in 1966. On September 26 coach Harry Gilmer suspended him for refusing to reenter the game against Atlanta the day before. Looney said he had a lump on his back and that, "I'm like a slave. I'm at their mercy. I have to play whenever they say. How can they suspend me? I told them I was hurt. He just looked at me and said I wasn't hurt."

Public Problems

Looney and rookie end Joe Flynn, roommates at training camp at Cranbrook, were in a pileup with a cop in the parking lot of the Golden Griddle Pancake House in Royal Oak at 3 a.m. August 2, 1965. Apparently there had been an argument inside over whether Looney's party had paid their bill. Witnesses said he hit a bottle against a wall. Five police officers showed up, but no charges were filed. Gilmore fined Looney $250. Flynn didn't make the team.

Six weeks later the owner of the Driftwood Lounge in Redford said Looney was in a shouting match with a woman at the bar who claimed he swore at her and threw a drink before she retaliated by throwing one herself. Lions Daryl Sanders, Tom Nowatzke, and Jim Simon also were there.

CALL WESTERN UNION

Then there was the time Gilmer asked Looney to take in a play for quarterback Milt Plum. "If you want a messenger, call Western Union!" Looney said. He was off on another suspension. It wasn't long before he drifted out of football and wound up in India studying Far East culture and religion under a guru. Looney was living the life of a hermit in Texas when he died late in 1988 in a motorcycle accident.

2

BARNSTORMERS

Debut 'Up North'

Traverse City is a popular resort area in Michigan's northwest lower peninsula, and our Lions basketball team would go up there for fund-raisers. We'd play a game on Thursday night, Friday night, and two on Saturday. It was the continuation of a long-standing informal association between the Lions and the city—which was the site of the team's first public appearance, September 15, 1934.

The franchise—recently transferred from Portsmouth, Ohio—played the Traverse City Athletic Club at the new 13th Street Athletic Park in an exhibition game that was a feature attraction of the American Legion convention. Coach Potsy Clark of the Lions had a squad of 33 players, and the team was about to sign another, All-America center Chuck Bernard of the University of Michigan. He was working at a Ford factory in the Detroit area. The Boston Redskins wanted him to play for them. Eight of the Lions were from Michigan colleges and universities.

Our team in 2004 had a training camp roster of 90 players, and 16 of them were under six feet tall with a dozen being at least 6-5. And there were 18 who weighed at least 300 pounds, topped by a couple at 335. Compare that with the 33 Lions on that 1934 roster: 11 were under six foot; the biggest was 6-5, 240-pound tackle Jesse Clark of Hillsdale College; the next biggest was 6-4, 210-pound tackle Jack Johnson from the University of Utah.

During the trip to Traverse City, Tommy Emmet was the Lions public relations director, and he had to make a lot of the arrangements. He made sure to bring "Grid" and "Iron" from home. They were lions cubs presented to the team by the Detroit Zoo.

Champs Show Off Out West

Nowadays we play four exhibition games and a 16-game season, and fans also get plenty of opportunities to see us on TV. But in those early days, the only way to see the team was to go in person. The Lions had a chance to make a barnstorming trip out west after the 1934 season, "but we didn't go because we failed to win," Potsy Clark told Bob Murphy of the *Detroit Times* in November 1935. "Now it's different. The boys want the trip, and both Mr. Richards [team owner George Richards] and I want them to have it."

Because of their NFL championship in 1935, interest was high, and various all-star teams were coming out of the woodwork to play the Lions during the long swing west. But one of the stops proved to be a thorn in their side, a scheduled game December 29 in Ogden, Utah. The game never took place. The Lions warmed up at 1:40 p.m., but left the stadium when their opponents' equipment didn't show up. It finally arrived, but the Lions had just left. There already were 800 spectators in the stands, and they were given refunds. However, the next day's headline in the *Salt Lake City Telegram* read: 'Pro champs face suit after Ogden grid fiasco.' That was a day after the *Ogden Standard-Examiner* proclaimed: 'Record crowd looms for Utah's first pro grid game.'

Things were a bit better on New Year's Day 1936, though, as the Lions beat an all-star team 33-0 at Denver University Stadium before a crowd of 12,000. Twelve days after that they were in Los Angeles to play the Westwood Cubs in Gilmore Stadium. After cruising to a 54-0 lead, the Lions won 67-14. They had 17 first downs to just one for the opponent, and that one came on a penalty.

"It was hardly more than a brisk workout for the Detroit boys," said the story in the *Los Angeles Examiner*. Braven Dyer, writing in the *Los Angeles Times*, wrote, "The Detroit Lions are the greatest football squad that ever visited the far west."

The team stayed in southern California for a while, and on January 19 they beat Harry Edelson's All-Stars 42-7 in L.A. before 7,000 spectators. The following week, January 26 at Gilmore Stadium, they faced real NFL competition and edged the Green Bay Packers 10-3 before a turnout of 20,000. Ace Gutowsky had an 84-yard touchdown run, and Dutch Clark dropkicked a field goal for the Lions' points.

They weren't done yet. The Lions headed to Honolulu where, on February 9, they beat the Hawaii All-Stars, coached by Glenn "Pop" Warner, 30-6. Glenn Presnell returned a kickoff 96 yards for a touchdown for Detroit. The game was splashed in banner headlines in the *Honolulu Advertiser*, *Honolulu Star-Bulletin*, and *Nippu Jiji*—a Japanese language newspaper. (I remember in 2004 when Presnell died at age 99 and we put out a press release about it. He was the last surviving player from the first Lions team.)

3

BASEBALL BECKONED

HARDNOSED TITAN

I had a chance to play with Bruce Maher and quickly found out what a tough player he was. No one much figured Maher—with an eye also toward a possible baseball career—would make it with the Lions after being their 15th-round draft choice in 1959 out of the University of Detroit. The 5-11, 185-pounder hit .400 for U-D in the spring. Even his father, John, didn't sound all that confident. When Bruce was a star athlete at U-D, his dad was quoted as saying: "I want him to be a football player. I'd like him to be a good one. I'd even like him to be great one, but there aren't many of those. Probably he won't make it at all."

But when Bruce retired in the summer of 1970 after a 10-year National Football League career (the final two years with the New York Giants), he went out with a reputation as one of the toughest Lions ever. Epitomizing his grit was a photo in which he is shown up in the air, doubled over, with an opponent's foot embedded in his stomach. The five-foot-10, 190-pound defensive back had just blocked a kick. Perhaps he got his toughness from his father, who was an amateur boxer and all-state football player.

"I ain't hit him yet, but I haven't given up," his dad was quoted as saying during his son's collegiate years. "I'm waiting until he's old and in a wheelchair, and then I'm going to sneak up and belt him. It'll be the first time I have ever hit him."

I heard a story about him driving a car and getting into an altercation with a truck driver. The guy got out of his truck with a tire iron, but when it was all over, that driver was on the ground and didn't have a chance to use the bar or his fists. Bruce supposedly worked him over pretty good.

A big story on campus in 1959 was whether Maher would turn pro in football or baseball. He spent three months with the Detroit Tigers' Durham team in the Class B Carolina League, but gave up that idea after only appearing in a dozen games as a spare outfielder. He had five hits in a .217 average. George Puscas of the *Free Press*

Bruce Maher was a star baseball player, as well as football player, at the University of Detroit and nearly opted to play pro baseball, but instead went on to a fine career with the Lions as a defensive back. *Photo courtesy of the Detroit Lions*

reported in November 1960 that Maher received $5,000 from the Tigers and could get $15,000 more if he were to leave the Lions and hit well at Triple-A Denver.

Also in the *Free Press*, Joe Falls quoted Maher as saying: "I don't want to be evasive, but let's say I like football in the fall and baseball in the spring. If you're good—I mean really good—you can make money in baseball. But if you're average in both sports, I think you can make more money in football."

The following spring *The Detroit News* published a photo of Tigers executive Rick Ferrell (later inducted into the Baseball Hall of Fame) tutoring Maher in Lakeland on catching.

As a Lion, he was noted for his diving, shoestring tackles and overall hard-nosed play. But before he earned that reputation, assistant coach Don Shula said, "In a year or two, Bruce could be of great value." One player said Maher hit so hard in training camp and "the only other guy who got away with that was Jimmy David." He never was in the Pro Bowl game, but he was the Lions' Most Valuable Player in 1965—and the Giants' MVP in 1968.

Raymond Berry, the Baltimore Colts receiver who went on to become an NFL Hall of Fame member, said he had wished Maher would have hit .380 and stolen 69 bases in baseball so that he wouldn't have become a football player. "Any way way to keep him out of football," Berry said. "That fellow tackles too hard."

Maher retired to become a sales manager for a company in Detroit. "I still feel I have a couple of good years left," he said. "But as my father once said, 'Better to say you don't need them than to have them tell you.'"

WICKED CURVEBALL

If Bobby Layne hadn't become a Hall of Fame quarterback for the Lions maybe he would have been a major league baseball player. Former major leaguer Randy Jackson said Layne had phenomenal baseball ability. Jackson, who played baseball with Layne at the University of Texas, played for several major league teams. He hit the last home run for the Brooklyn Dodgers and the first one for the Los Angeles Dodgers. Jackson was quoted in Irwin Cohen's April 1987 column in *Sports Fans' Journal*:

"Bobby was a pitcher and was something like 28-1 over his career at Texas. He never would have made it in the big leagues because he had a fantastic curveball but he never got it over. The batters in college would swing at it even if it bounced on the plate. He was a competitor, though. He'd win a game for you."

'LIGERS?'

The Lions, in all my years with them, always had a great relationship with baseball's Detroit Tigers—and, for that matter, all the athletes from the other pro teams in town. Tigers like Earl Wilson, Gates Brown, Norm Cash, Willie Horton, Al Kaline, and other athletes all ended up at banquets together or we'd run into each other, and also at the Lindell A.C., because it was a natural hangout for athletes. We were all close, especially after the riots of 1967 and 1968. All four pro teams really rallied together.

But I wonder how many people know that the Lions' owners in 1956 made a bid to buy the Tigers, offering $250,000. However, they needed "yes" votes from all 10 NFL owners and didn't get them. Four decades later, Mike Ilitch became the first double pro sports franchise owner in the city, taking on both the Tigers and hockey's Red Wings.

4

BASKETBALL GRIDDERS

PISTONS OVERTURES

I don't know if anyone realizes it, but Lem Barney and I both got a chance to play pro basketball with the Detroit Pistons, at least for a look. We played on an all-star team at Cobo Arena downtown. Pistons coach Bill van Breda Kolff (1969-1972) saw us and wanted us to try out. He said he wanted a "banger" and "We need you as an intimidator." Nothing came of it, though. That was when I was in my third year with the Lions.

DIAPERED LIONS

When I played charity basketball games with our Lions team, apparently it was a tradition that began nearly 30 years before I came to Detroit. Abe Kushner, a 126-pound Detroit Lions trainer, organized a basketball team in 1940 featuring mostly Lions players. It was called "Abie's Babies," and eventually the players wore diaper-like trunks with a baby bottle design on the front. The team barnstormed around the state. Tickets cost from 25-50 cents. Lions on the squad were Lloyd Cardwell, John Pingel, Alex Wojceichowicz, Chuck Hanneman, Bill Rogers, Cal Thomas, and Dwight "Paddlefoot" Sloan (who didn't stick with the Lions).

PROCEEDS FOR GOOD CAUSES

The tradition of Lions playing basketball games continued into the 1950s and 1960s. In 1955, Romeo High School held a charity fund-raising game to finance the $660 needed for a student's operation and for college scholarships. The game matched the school's varsity against mostly Lions. Among them were Lou Creekmur, Bob Hoernschemeyer, Jug Girard, Dorne Dibble, Lou Ane, Leon Hart,

Sonny Gandee, one of the Lions stars of the 1950s, plays here in one of the team's many charity basketball games. *Photo courtesy of the Detroit Lions*

Les Bingaman, and Sonny Gandee. Others on the Lions unit were ex-MSU quarterback Al Dorow of the Redskins and Don Lund of the Tigers.

The 1960 Lions also had a basketball team that performed charity exhibitions in the off-season. In February they played the Ionia Falstaff Independents at Ionia High School. The preliminary game matched the Ionia Reformatory against the Ionia State Hospital team. Players for Detroit were Jim Gibbons, Jerry Reichow, Nick Pietrosante, Howard Cassady, Terry Barr, Gary Lowe, Alex Karras, Darris McCord, and assistant GM Bud Erickson.

In another game, against River Rouge police and firefighters, the Lions were playing to benefit a widow with nine children whose husband was killed February 2 in a car crash. There also was a game in Berkley against that suburb's Class B recreation champion, Kelly's Appliances. It benefited the city's Babe Ruth baseball program.

BOSS SOURS ON BASKETBALL

A fight at an exhibition basketball game March 22, 1963, between Alex Karras of the Lions and a 20-year-old player from the opponent team from Belleville prompted GM Edwin Anderson to consider barring Lions from playing in off-season basketball games. Also that winter, the Lions played a team of Chicago Bears on a Friday night at Olympia Stadium in a game prior to an appearance by the Harlem Globetrotters.

There were quite a few incidents that I remember in which teammates were injured as a result of our basketball fund-raisers. I can recall being up in Bad Axe and severely twisting my ankle to the point where I had to go to the hospital and have X-rays. I can remember being in Canada and elbowing Herb Orvis across the eye. The bad part about that was that we had a problem getting emergency treatment.

There often were sprained ankles, or someone would have to get stitches from an inadvertent elbow, or they'd get a tooth knocked out. But we never had any severe knee injuries or anything like that which might have jeopardized our football careers.

5

'BIG BUCKS'

'WE DON'T RENEGOTIATE'

Getting paid a bonus for doing well wasn't necessarily going to happen, as I soon found out. My first three years in the league my contracts were for $16,000; $17,000; and $18,000. I made the Pro Bowl team each of the first two years and so I went in to talk to Russ Thomas, the general manager, about renegotiating. Quite naturally, being the businessman he was, he said, "We don't renegotiate contracts."

I went on to make the Pro Bowl again and thought I'd get a healthy new contract. I went in to ask for $40,000, and Russ said that was more than double what I was making. I held out for a while and when I did sign it was for a little less than $40,000, so I never got what I wanted, but I did hold out of training camp in order to get a better contract to sign.

It view of that, it was interesting to learn of old Lions center Vince Banonis, who didn't play for the team until 1951, although he was an All-American at the University of Detroit in 1941 (as chosen by *Collier's* magazine) and was drafted by the Chicago Cardinals as their No. 1 draft choice. They offered him $2,500. There was no bonus for signing, just a simple contract. Banonis, according to the Fred Smith column in the January 1988 issue of *Sports Fans' Journal*, went to his UD (and later Lions) coach, Gus Dorais, and asked if he thought he could get $2,600. Dorais said to try it, and Banonis sent the contract back with the notation that he wanted $100 more. The Cardinals agreed with the request, which by today's standards would be laughable for a No. 1 draft pick. Banonis, who also served in the military in WWII, had a 12-year NFL career.

6

BREAKING BARRIERS

TIMES CHANGING

The first African-American player signed by the Lions was Melvin Harold Groomes, a six-foot, 172-pound halfback from the University of Indiana. He joined the squad in 1948, the same year another African-American player, Bob Mann (whom I had heard about) became a Lion. Mann was an end from the University of Michigan. Both played two years with the team. Mann was traded to the New York Bulldogs for a quarterback named Bobby Layne.

FOOTBALL WRITERS OPEN DOOR

When the Lions started signing a few African-American players to their roster after WWII, the *Michigan Chronicle*, sold primarily in the predominantly black neighborhoods of Detroit, took more interest in covering the team, and in 1948, sports editor Bill Matney became a regular in the Briggs Stadium press box, as did Frank Saunders from the *Chronicle* two decades later. Saunders and I often were at the same sports dinners and we were of similar age, and he always found me. He wrote a few articles on me.

Matney, though, was the pioneer. "The first time this writer ever sat in the Briggs Stadium was last year when he covered the home football games of the Lions," Matney wrote in his "Jumpin the Grid" column in September 1949. "Last year I had the pleasure of joining the Football Writers Association of America as a full member as a member in good standing. I am accorded full privileges of a football writer in any grid press box in the nation.

"Until last year, there were no Negroes in that organization. I do not think there are any other Negro writers in the association. The presence of a Negro in the Briggs Stadium press box last winter did not wreak any hardships upon the association.

Other writers greeted us cordially. Most of the local writers are swell fellows anyway."

The next year Matney, suggesting racism as the reason, would be very critical of the Lions' trade of Mann, who refused to take a $1,500 salary cut in 1950 (from a salary of $7,500) after leading the league with 1,015 yards receiving. He said he was railroaded out of the league and would push his case with Commissioner Bert Bell.

The New York Yankees got Mann and a fifth-round draft pick August 5, 1950, in exchange for Layne. Four months earlier Detroit had sent fullback Camp Wilson to New York in a straight trade for Layne, but when Wilson retired, the Lions had to come up with another player. New York wanted fullback Johnny Panelli. Mann's salary dispute, though, apparently made him vulnerable. The Yankees waived him and the other 12 teams passed on him.

"We traded Mann in good faith, and if he wasn't good enough to make the team it wasn't our fault," Lions PR man Nick Kerbawy said in a November 1, 1950, *Free Press* article. Coach Red Strader of the Yankees said Mann, at 168 pounds, was too small and not versatile enough. Mann, who caught 66 passes in 1949, suddenly found himself going to an unemployment compensation hearing. The former Michigan star, though, latched on with Green Bay in 1950 and lasted through the 1953 season with the Packers.

7

COACH CAROUSEL

The Lions have had nearly two dozen head coaches in their history (and about 200 assistants), starting in 1929 with Hal Griffen, when they were the Portsmouth Spartans. They've had their good ones and not-so-good ones, and some who may have been good but never had the talent with which to work. When Detroit went through numerous mediocre-to-poor seasons, the coaches with "five-year" plans to turn things around rarely got more than three years to prove themselves. There was a revolving door of coaches. Though I didn't know the earlier ones, because of my long tenure in Detroit—including time in the Lions radio booth—I felt an obligation to learn about some of those earlier coaches in order to supplement my first-hand knowledge of the later ones.

No Patsy

The first Lions coach, Potsy Clark (1931-1936, 1940), and I had one thing in common, we both played in the Big Ten—many generations apart. He was an All-America quarterback at the University of Illinois in 1914. He quit his job as coach at the Colorado School of Mines to take the Lions coaching job on March 27, 1934 (although he had been coaching the Portsmouth, Ohio, Spartans before the team was put up for sale).

A dozen years before he became the Spartans' coach, Clark was playing for the 89th Division football team, leading it to the American Expeditionary Forces championship in Paris, March 29, 1919, right after World War I. His team defeated the 36th Division 14-6. Clark scored both touchdowns (one on a 65-yard run) and kicked both extra points.

He wasn't exactly a household name in Detroit. The *Polish Daily Record*, in its story about the city getting the franchise, called him "Patsy" Clark. But Clark didn't waste time getting friendly with the local news media. By the end of August he was booked as a guest on the Charley Gehringer program at 7:45 p.m. on radio station

Although Hal Griffen was coach of the Lions predecessors in Portsmouth, Ohio, Potsy Clark (shown here) took over the job when the Spartans became the Detroit Lions. *Photo courtesy of the Detroit Lions*

WJR. Gehringer was the great Detroit Tigers second baseman, who would eventually go into the Baseball Hall of Fame. Clark also wrote newspaper columns and, in October 1934, the slick *American Legion Monthly* magazine published his article headlined, "Our Other National Game".

It didn't seem to matter whether he was talking to his big-name stars or the last guy on the bench, Clark had no qualms about putting them on the spot just to show who was in charge. As an example, there was the time at training camp in August 1936 when, according to Tod Rockwell's story in the *Free Press*, Potsy, at a team meeting, asked his superstar back, Dutch Clark, what a touchdown was.

"It's the thing you get when you…" Dutch started to say in response, before Potsy interrupted him and asked a smirking Glenn Presnell, another superstar back, what a TD was.

"Well, coach, a touchdown is scored when…" Presnell said, before also getting interrupted by his coach, who said he didn't ask him "when" it was scored, but what it was.

Rookie quarterback Reino Nori didn't answer, either. Then the little trainer, Abe Kushner, chimed in: "A touchdown is the principal score of the game. It is made by carrying the ball on, above, or across the opponent's goal line, or by completing a forward pass in the opponent's end zone; also, by legally recovering the ball on or in the end zone of the opponent."

"Well, I'll swear!" declared the coach. "He's the only guy in the room who doesn't need to know the rules and he's the only guy here who knows 'em. This class is now dismissed—but not until each and every one of you guys writes out what Abe said 10 times."

CONTRASTING CLARKS

When Potsy Clark was coaching the Lions of the mid-1930s and Dutch Clark was his superstar quarterback, things were very in sync. It must have been kind of strange on September 25, 1940, when coach Dutch Clark's Cleveland Rams were in Detroit to face the Lions of Potsy Clark, who had returned after three years to coach the team again.

"It was a great football combination," *Times* sports columnist Bob Murphy wrote of the two men's time in Detroit. "Many, many times I've seen Potsy Clark light up like a proud father when he spoke of the Dutchman. And I don't believe Dutch Clark ever had more respect for any man than he has for Potsy Clark.

"In a way, the Clarks are as different as broccoli and borscht. Potsy is a personality guy plus. Dutch is more the country bumpkin type. Potsy will sit up half the night, when he's not working, with a group telling stories and singing old time songs. Dutch prefers to don his slippers and read Wild West stories."

'PROFESSOR' FORGETS DOG

There's a funny story about one of the old Lions coaches, Gus Henderson, and a dog and it brought to mind my own dog story. My first dog was a German shepherd named "Segeede." She had three sets of 15 puppies. I had nine kids and 45 pups.

One of my teammates, Craig Cotton, came to my house one day and my dog started heading menacingly toward him and he got worried. I told him he better say his name. Finally, I had to say it and then the dog was friendly to him. We gave the pups to players, but most went to police in Minnesota. I used to take the dog back to Minnesota during training camp.

Dutch Clark coached the Lions in 1937 and 1938, but got tired of interference from team owner Dick Richards and quit after the 1938 season. On December 27, Richards brought in Henderson, whose record at Southern Cal was 40-7. He had 29 years of coaching experience, including at Tulsa and for the minor league Los

Angeles Bulldogs, who won 17 in a row under his tutelage. Also, he coached three high school championship teams in Seattle.

Southern California has been one of Notre Dame's great rivals since the days of Henderson, who introduced intersectional games against such prominent teams from the Midwest and East.

The Lions trained at Cranbrook Institute in the posh suburb of Bloomfield Hills in 1939. *Detroit News* columnist H.C.L. Jackson wrote of Henderson:

"Cranbrook, incidentally, seems a fitting background for Coach Henderson. In fact, you'd rather expect to see him staying on and teaching a course in, say, medieval history. He looks far more like a professor than a football coach."

Jackson related a story about Henderson retrieving a friend's $125 Irish setter from Pontiac because he was out in that direction anyway. On the way home, driving down Woodward Avenue on a rainy day, he picked up a woman at a bus stop to give her a lift. The dog started barking, and the woman said her brother loved dogs and could Gus please take her all the way home so her brother could see the dog. He did, and later the brother offered him a beer.

"I don't drink beer," said Henderson (who's late father, John P. Henderson, was a founder of the American Anti-Saloon League).

"How's for a snort of likker?" the woman's brother asked.

Despite his dad's anti-booze stance, Gus said yes and he'd take it straight. The man's sister, though, wanted it with ginger ale and he didn't have any, so Henderson volunteered to go find a drug store to get some, leaving the dog behind. He didn't know the neighborhood and drove around a lot before finding a store and getting the ginger ale. But upon leaving he realized all the houses in the area were cookie-cutter alike. "He never did find the house and so never got his friend's dog back," Jackson wrote.

It must have been a trying first month for Henderson. His dad, who was a banker in Oberlin, Ohio, and an educator, died August 5, 1939, in a Cleveland hospital at the age of 77.

BIG NAMES OPT OUT

Whenever the Lions went through one of their coaching changes, newspaper speculation about possible successors always was rife. Big names abounded in the "candidate" pool. When owner Fred Mandel fired Potsy Clark on November 28, 1940, his first choice as a replacement was Gus Dorais, the coach and athletic director at the University of Detroit for 18 years. Another possibility was Frank Leahy of Boston College, who was offered the job but declined.

Joseph Sheeketsky, a Detroiter who was the coach at Holy Cross, was another candidate, and two former star Michigan quarterbacks were mentioned, as well: Harry Newman and Benny Friedman. Clark, meanwhile, signed on as head coach and public relations director for Grand Rapids Junior College.

Despite the "big names" bandied about, Mandel announced February 17, 1941, that 35-year-old William Edwards of Western Reserve University in Cleveland would be the new coach and would bring his assistant, Roy Miller, with him. Western Reserve had beaten Arizona State 26-13 in the 1940 Sun Bowl. It posted a 40-6-2 record under Edwards, with three unbeaten seasons.

A *United Press* story the day after the announcement said it was puzzling that Edwards took the job in view of Detroit being "the graveyard of coaches in professional circles." (That could have been a tag line 30 years later, as well.) It had to take a sizeable offer, it speculated, to improve on his $4,200-a-year salary. Edwards was the fifth Lions coach in five years. A *Detroit News* article said 32 college and three pro teams changed coaches after the 1940 season.

Miller headed to Detroit in his car that June but skidded into a bridge near Delaware, Ohio, and fractured his knee. His in-laws also were hurt in the accident. Another newcomer to the Lions was trainer Al Sawdy of the Fostoria Red Birds of the Ohio State League. He had worked with Edwards at Fostoria High School.

TUNNEL PROMOTION

Edwards never made it through the following season. Mandel fired him October 4, 1942. Backfield coach John Karcis was walking down the runway from the field after the Lions' 28-7 loss at home against Brooklyn and met Mandel, who, according to *The News*, asked Karcis, "How would you like to take charge of this club?"

Karcis, who said he was "feeling pretty low because our club had taken another beating and had looked pretty bad, too," said he "was never more surprised in my life" and couldn't turn down such an offer. However, he didn't want to undermine Edwards, and Mandel said he'd take care of it. Moments later Mandel sat in a closed-door meeting and fired Edwards and Miller, then appointed John Weithe as line coach and Lloyd Cardwell as backfield coach under Karcis.

"I hated to make a switch at this time, but something had to be done to get us out of the rut," said Mandel, who had watched his team get shut out the first two games, 13-0 to the Chicago Cardinals away and 14-0 to the Cleveland Rams at home.

BACKYARD CHOICE

The Lions lost their eight other games in 1942 under Karcis to finish 0-11 and, on Christmas Eve, Mandel went to the team's own back yard and offered the job to Dorais, coach and athletic director at UD. On January 10, 1943, the former Notre Dame University playing legend (the front end of the Dorais-to-Knute Rockne passing combination) ended his 18-year run at UD to accept the job.

According to newspaper stories, he would be paid $7,500 if the league discontinued the 1943 season because of the war, or $12,000 if operations continued. Bob Sieger of *The News* said the contract was for five years. Dorais became the seventh coach of the team and fourth since Mandel took over just three years earlier.

"This is the most important move the Lions have ever made," Mandel said.

Two months later, Dorais, who also was a city councilman, had a dizzy spell in the washroom of the Detroit Athletic Club and hit his head on the tile floor, fracturing his skull. He was taken to Ford Hospital, but it turned out not to be serious and he was prescribed rest and quiet. Several years earlier he had fractured his skull falling on icy steps.

FRIEND TO ALL

Bo McMillin, who had a 12-24 record in his three seasons (1948-1950) as Lions coach, died of cancer in Bloomington, Indiana, March 31, 1952. Edgar Hayes of the *Detroit Times* ran this Will Rogers-esque quote from McMillin: "There are a million people in the world I think I can call a friend, but I can't think of a single person I could call an enemy."

METICULOUS—AND SUPERSTITIOUS

The closest coach I knew with the work ethic of Buddy Parker was Bobby Ross (1997-2000). Bobby was a workaholic who'd have the coaches in at 6 a.m. Saturday. He studied films and broke everything down. He didn't want to leave a stone unturned. He might have left due to burnout.

Old-time Lions fans I've spoken with over the years often spoke reverently about Parker, who was the coach of the championship 1952 and 1953 Lions, and the runner-up 1954 team. A coach's strong work ethic doesn't always translate into victories and championships, but it certainly did for Parker, who "dies for Detroit every week," declared a big feature article on him in the November 13, 1954, edition of the *Saturday Evening Post*. The story, by Stanley Frank, said Parker averaged six hours a day analyzing film, one frame at a time.

"He may stare at a frame for 20 minutes in stupefying silence, jot on a blackboard the cabalistic crosses and circles of a formation, then sink into another deep trance while he scrutinized the diagram," Frank wrote, adding that sometimes it took Parker two days to review a single quarter of a game, during which the ball was in play five minutes.

Once he got a haircut at the Hotel Seward barbershop. The Lions won the next game, and so thereafter Parker got all his haircuts there. Also, he was apprehensive about flying unless sports editor Bob McClelland of the *Times* sat in the window seat next to him.

"For all his superstitions," Frank wrote, "Parker is essentially a down-to-earth meat-and-potatoes type of coach. He resorts to less technical double-talk than practically any other coach you are likely to encounter. The Lions have only 20 basic

Buddy Parker didn't miss a detail in charting plays for the Lions, and his precise parsing of plays certainly paid off as can be seen in this photo of the Lions carrying him off the field after their championship victory in 1952 over the Cleveland Browns. *Photo courtesy of the Detroit Lions*

plays, or about 50 in all with variations, and they seldom use more than half their repertory in any given game." By comparison, he said, the Bears had 300 plays.

Quarterback Bobby Layne said Parker "was the smartest coach I was ever around. He was able to do things with a pencil and paper that people do with computers today. No one was better at grading a film."

Party Squelcher

Parker wasn't known as a tough disciplinarian, but even he decided to put his foot down on his party-minded players when they were in Los Angeles in 1953 for an important game against the Rams. He issued orders for a strict midnight curfew and installed a nightly bed check. The move was not punitive, *News* writer Watson Spoelstra wrote, but rather "designed to end after-dark sightseeing by his players."

Tigers president Spike Briggs was with the team on that trip, the newspaper reported, to learn first hand the high cost of transporting athletes to the West Coast, since major league baseball expected to expand soon to California.

Runner-up Depression

When the Lions lost the 1954 championship to the Cleveland Browns, thus missing a chance for three consecutive titles, Parker, according to Layne, had a few drinks and went into his basement game room "and took a pocket knife and slashed his portrait painting."

Sole Survivor Says No Thanks

My coach, Joe Schmidt, said if his assistants were being fired, he'd go, too. And that's what he did after the 1972 season. I respected that. But that wasn't the first time something like that happened. George Wilson did the same thing a couple days before Christmas in 1964. He was the only one who survived a coaching staff housecleaning and he had had two years to run on a three-year, $40,000-per-year contract. But two days after his assistants all got the axe following complaints from players about the team's dull offense and poor use of skills, he decided he had no business sticking around.

Cowboy Gear a Trademark

One of my teammates, Horace King, used to always wear a cowboy hat and boots. That was a couple decades after coach Harry Gilmer left the Vikings for Detroit and started a trend of just about everyone on the Lions wearing his trademark cowboy hat and boots. George Puscas of the *Free Press* quoted him as saying someone razzed one of the Vikings about it and was reminded that one player who DIDN'T join those who began wearing the apparel was traded.

Horses 'Stay on Their Feet'

Gilmore was a horse lover. "I just happen to like horses," he said, "not to ride so much, but they're just something you can have and maybe talk to if you want to say this is mine." He had two horses he got from Steelers owner Art Rooney and "I'll have to find a place for them.... They're not much for speed, but they stay on their feet." (Russ Thomas and Tom Nowatzke also owned horses then.)

Just Hold It

News columnist Doc Greene also wrote a Gilmore feature and said when Gilmore was in the All-Star game, his only job was to hold the ball for Lou Groza's kicks. "In the first practice I asked, "Kickers like the ball held different ways... tilted... straight up... laces away... laces front. How do you like it, Lou?" Gilmore said. To that, Groza replied, "Put it down."

Thick Files

In Gilmore's days, and to this day, Henry Ford Hospital is where we'd go for examinations. Dr. Edwin Guise was the team physician, and I had the thickest file of anyone. I remember once sitting outside his door and listening to him read all the crap from my file. He was talking about my ankles, which always were bad because of people hitting me low. I don't think the Lions could have traded me because I would have failed the physicals of the other teams.

Gilmore went to Ford Hospital for an examination in June 1965 and, according to the *Free Press* article by Mark Beltaire, the result came back with the name smeared and illegible. The coach later had the report on his desk and assistants glanced at it and were shocked to read about a bad sacroiliac, calcium deposits on both knees, chipped ankle, etc. "Were they relieved when they found out it was just me and not a player," Gilmore said.

Keep'n 'Em Loose

We had two "fans" coaches when I played with the Lions, assistants Chuck Knox (1967-1972) and John North (1965-1972). We called North "Threads," because he thought he was sharply dressed but really wasn't. He was my coach. Those two were like Frick and Frack. Knox used to call North "Skippy," meaning he should have a leash on because he had to be led around or he'd get lost. Those two kept us really loose and laughing. Those two were the life of the party when they got together.

To me, Knox was one of the best coaches I ever had, even though he coached the line. I thought of him as a blocking tight end. You could tell he was going to be a success because of his rapport with the ballplayers. To this day I have a lot of respect for him. At one point I almost considered going to Los Angeles and playing for him when he was the coach there, but I decided not to.

KEEP'N 'EM IN STEP

The Lions went through many head coaches in the 1970s and 1980s and, of course, each had his own philosophy of how things should be done. Rick Forzano (1974-1976) was former coach at the U.S. Naval Academy and in 1974 was a Lions assistant when coach Don McCafferty died unexpectedly in the off-season. Forzano replaced him, and his approach was one of military-type discipline—although he was an easy-going quipper with the press.

We knew what to expect. He had a hard time with guys like Herb Orvis, who asked what it would take to be traded. The coach said to simply ask him and he would look to the right people to get that accomplished. So Herb asked to be traded, and when nothing was done within a few weeks, in a meeting I was at he called Forzano a liar because nobody had done anything about getting him out of here. He basically looked at Rick and said what does a man have to do to get released by this organization? A short time later Orvis was traded to the Colts.

We would go through five-hour practices with one water break, and that didn't set well with the guys (and wouldn't be allowed nowadays) and some were walking out of camp. Since I had been elected captain, I had to try to deal with these problems. The players rebelled by having me march them down in uniform in military formation. We came to a halt just before we got to the gate at Cranbrook and I went to Forzano and saluted him and told him we were "All present and accounted for, sir!" That was my routine.

The five-hour practices came to a halt. Forzano's philosophy didn't work with us. Among his ideas was not to fly out to Oakland, California, until two or three days before our game against the Raiders. It wasn't necessary to get acclimated, he said, because it was proven that jet lag didn't take effect until two days after you arrived. So he figured we could get in there and play the game and the jet lag wouldn't hit us until the following day. That didn't last long after we lost 35-13. Like many who came before him, and after, Forzano got fired when the Lions couldn't rise above mediocrity.

HEART BETRAYS 'PLAYER'S COACH'

A week after Joe Schmidt resigned in January 1973 after six years as Lions head coach, team owner William Clay Ford hired Don McCafferty, a man with plenty of credentials, including a Super Bowl championship ring. It could have been a pivotal move in team history. We thought it would be a turning point for us. But as fate would have it, the move was the beginning of a head-coach merry-go-round that never did bring the Lions out of their long-time doldrums.

Perhaps McCafferty could have developed the Lions into a Super Bowl team as he had done with the Baltimore Colts in the 1970 season. They beat the Dallas Cowboys in the big game in January of 1971. But he suffered a heart attack while working in his yard in July 1974 and died without regaining consciousness. NFL players were on strike at the time, and the players cancelled their meeting as soon as they learned of the tragedy. McCafferty, for whom I had a lot of respect, was "a player's coach," said Ed Flanagan, the team's captain and player's union representative.

General manager Russ Thomas said the 53-year-old McCafferty passed his physical in May without any sign of heart trouble. "His death is a serious loss to the sport, a serious loss to the town, and a serious loss to our football team," Thomas said. NFL commissioner Pete Rozelle said of McCafferty: "There probably never was a coach who had a closer relationship with his players."

The Lions struggled in McCafferty's lone year in charge, posting a 6-7-1 record. His record with Baltimore was 22-10-2, including an 11-2-1 mark in the 1970 season that ended with the Super Bowl triumph. The Colts were 10-4-1 the next season, but five games into the 1972 season they were off to a 1-4 start and he was fired by general manager Joe Thomas, who himself was fired later in the year.

McCafferty came into Detroit with a nickname of "Easy Rider" for purportedly being an easy coach. He denied being easy on his players, saying the tag was put on him by the news media a few years earlier, and "it's been hard to shake."

After a particularly bad loss, 20-0, in November 1973 to the Washington Redskins, McCafferty said: "We stunk out the joint, period. It was embarrassing.... We've got some losers on this ball club, and they won't be around next year."

GREAT ANTICIPATION

Joe Schmidt (LB, 1953-1965; Coach, 1967-1972) probably was the best head coach I ever played for. He knew what you were thinking before you thought it. He knew what you were going to say before you said it. Anything you say, he'd been there, done that. He'd say he's done it all, probably because as a collegian at Pittsburgh and a legendary Lions linebacker (1953-1965), he probably did. Maybe he was such a great player because he knew what was going to happen before it did and was able to anticipate where to make the play.

He was just a guy who liked to see you go out and give your all. That's all he asked of you. In the long run, he may not have gotten a shot or what he needed to be able to do what he wanted to do. He was great to work with because of his work ethic and what he believed in to get the job done.

That work ethic obviously carried over from his playing days when he set the standard for linebacker play and became a perennial All-Pro. When former Lions assistant coach Don Shula went to Baltimore as the Colts' head coach, Shula said from his own charting of rivals against defenses, he found that in 1961 Schmidt was guilty of only seven mistakes in judgment or execution out of 890 plays over 14 games.

Schmidt, an unidentified Lions assistant coach once said, Schmidt was "everything everybody wants to see in an athlete. He's superior, the best on the field and just as commendable away from it. He's what you think of when you mention 'ideal' athletes." That's what made his 1963 punishment for betting on a game all the more demoralizing.

Schmidt and several other teammates were fined $2,000 by NFL commissioner Pete Rozelle in 1963 for betting $50 each that Green Bay would beat the New York Giants in the 1962 championship game. Alex Karras, meanwhile, was suspended for the entire season for various infractions.

"I saw him yesterday," coach George Wilson said after Schmidt was fined. "He's really taking this thing hard. He's not the same Joe. I've seen teams fall completely apart after something like this happens to them."

Board member William Clay Ford, soon to take over ownership of the team, said Schmidt was "a fellow of intense pride, and this thing really hurt him. I know him well, but even I have to wonder how much effect this will have on him in the long run." But assistant coach Scooter McLean said Schmidt "is going to be all the tougher, because he's going to want to prove all over again the kind of man he is. And he's a real man. On top of the football and everything else, he's as fine a man as you'll find anywhere."

Joe Schmidt's ability to anticipate what was going to happen probably helped make him a great player and then also served him well in his days as Detroit's coach.
Photo courtesy of the Detroit Lions

8

CONNIVING AND CONSPIRACY

BAD TAX WRITE-OFFS

There might not have been anything fishy about them, but there were a couple investments I made that must have made the ghost of P.T. Barnum chuckle. One involved cattle. I owned some in Kansas at one time, a special breed that were to be used for artificial insemination. They cost me between $5,000 and $8,000 a head, and I wanted them for a tax shelter. But soon after I invested $20,000, the government disallowed any tax write-off for them. I did get a nice box of steaks, though. It amounted to about $1,000 a steak.

Another bad tax "write-off" investment I made was to put money in the 1974 British movie, *The Land That Time Forgot*, with Doug McClure. I was told it would be a sure money-loser; it wouldn't make a penny, which is what I was looking for. I even went to England to watch some filming and I met McClure. Wouldn't you know it, it was a big hit. Instead of a tax write-off, I got dividends—a couple dollars here and a couple there.

IDENTITY THEFT

Regardless of the era, there have been and probably always will be scam artists, connivers in and around the game of football. There was the time that coach Rick Forzano was convinced a woman was Shirley Temple Black, the former child movie superstar turned U.S. ambassador. It wasn't her, but she got invited down to the sidelines for a game.

And there would be people who'd try to steal your identity. There were people who thought I lived in Utica, because there was a guy there who professed to being Charlie Sanders.

Special Enticements

Chicago Bears owner George Halas seemed like he was around forever. He was still there when I was with the Lions in the 1970s. About 25 years earlier he drafted a college star named Clyde "Bulldog" Turner of Hardin-Simmons, who became an NFL superstar. It had been alleged that Lions owner Dick Richards had given Turner $100 not to sign with any team, and Richards also would pay extensive dental bills for him.

Before the NFL gave final official sanction to the Lions' transfer of ownership that year from Richards to Fred Mandel, in April it fined Richards $5,300 for player tampering. Turner had filled out the league questionnaire, something that players aren't supposed to do if they don't plan on playing professionally. At the bottom of the sheet, he wrote that he didn't wish to play pro ball. Halas detected from that that Turner did, in fact, did want to play, and so he drafted him. Coach Gus Henderson of the Lions, meanwhile, didn't draft him because of Turner's note. That decision reportedly broke Richards and Henderson apart and helped lead to the coach's dismissal.

'Radiator Rent'

I've seen the movie, *Knute Rockne, All-American* a few times, and until recently it didn't dawn on me that the Gus Dorais portrayed in the movie was the same quarterback who went on to become University of Detroit and ultimately Detroit Lions football coach. In the movie, he and Rockne worked on the forward pass while lifeguards at Cedar Pointe Amusement Park in Ohio, and it revolutionized the game.

However, something the two aren't remembered for is a scheme they hatched while rooming together in a cellar apartment. They teamed on an offbeat scam to make money, according to Arthur Dailey in a *New York Times* column in 1945. Dorais was the "front man," Dailey wrote. "He'd knock on the door and ask solemnly if the 'radiator rent' was paid. If not, he'd regretfully summon his accomplice, and Rock would dismantle the radiator with a huge wrench. It was a profitable business until the authorities got wind of it. The firm was dissolved quickly."

Dorais was one of the honorary pallbearers at Rockne's funeral in South Bend, Indiana, after Rockne was killed in a plane crash in Kansas in 1931.

Extortion Plot

Kobe Bryant of the Los Angeles Lakers was the center of attention in the 2004 basketball season for allegedly raping a woman in a Colorado hotel room. The

Lions coach Gus Dorais, right, seen here in 1943 with line coach Joe Bach, had an off-the-wall scheme to make money with teammate Knute Rockne during their days at Notre Dame. *Photo courtesy of the Detroit Lions*

Conniving and Conspiracy

matter was settled out of court, but athletes always have been vulnerable to such situations.

A half-century ago, NFL stars were in the limelight as much as today, and that made them a target of criminals. Tackle Lou Creekmur was the victim of an extortion plot in October 1950 that, had it happened today, would be plastered all over television, with gossip reporters trying to dig up any bit of lurid information, be it truth or rumor. Creekmur denied knowledge of the plot. Detroit police arrested two men and one woman and held them on conspiracy charges under bonds totaling $80,000.

The story in *The Detroit News* said the plot involved a 20-year-old woman who the alleged conspirators threatened into claiming the Lions player raped her after a party. Creekmur said he didn't know her and wasn't at any party. One of the suspects in the shakedown conspiracy also was a suspect in the 1945 murder of senator Warren G. Hooper, who had been scheduled to testify in a legislative graft case.

9

CUP OF COFFEE

SPEED WASN'T ENOUGH

In baseball when a player made it to the major leagues, but only briefly, it's said he had a "cup of coffee" in the bigs. Football has no such colorful expression, but that one would fit just as well. I remember coach Wayne Fontes saying in training camp one year that Slip Watkins was someone we'd all hear from because he was an Olympic sprinter with world-class speed. He didn't make it, though. He could run, but he couldn't catch. Another prospect like that was Renaldo Nehemiah, an Olympic sprinter and hurdler. There were, however, a couple Olympians who did make it and some others with special skills who had a short taste of the NFL.

DECATHLON CHAMP

Although end Glenn Morris played for the Lions briefly in 1940 (and also in the American Football League that year), it was four years earlier that coach Potsy Clark thought he would come to Detroit for a tryout. Morris was the Olympic decathlon champion. "It looks like Morris has decided not to risk his amateur athletic standing," Clark told the *Detroit Times*.

OLYMPIC HURDLER

Doc Greene of *The News* was in Rome in September 1960 to cover the summer Olympics and wrote a feature on Glenn Davis, the 400-meter hurdler from Ohio State who hoped to latch on to the Lions as a free agent. "I don't want to get hurt," the 165-pounder said. "My trouble when I played football before was I always wanted to run over everybody and I wasn't big enough. I'm in perfect physical condition now. I ran 15 220s in 25 seconds the other day getting ready. No, I don't think there's anybody in pro football who could catch me except maybe Dale

Mitchell of Cleveland." Davis hadn't played football since high school, but he made it with the Lions in 1960 and 1961.

He set the world record 400-meter hurdle time of 49.2 seconds and the Olympic mark of 49.3.

MIGHTY MITE

Everyone seemed to be excited about Reino Nori at training camp in 1936. He didn't make the team until the next year, but the mighty mite back was traded to the Brooklyn Dodgers. He played with them in 1937 after coach Potsy Clark left Detroit to take over the reins in Brooklyn. The following year Nori closed out his brief NFL career playing for the Chicago Bears.

"Nori is faster than Ernie Caddel," Clark said in a story by Bob Murphy of the *Detroit Times* in August 1936. "He looks to be one of the most glittering Lion recruits in camp." Another sports writer, Tod Rockwell of the *Detroit Free Press*, called Nori a "half pint" and said, "He looked like he ought to be carrying the water bucket."

Clark was enamored with Nori at Brooklyn, saying there: "He has everything I could wish for in a quarterback. He is an alert field general, spots even the slightest weaknesses in the enemy defense, and then he knows exactly what to do about it. He is one of the fastest men on our squad, and he is hard to catch in a broken field." Clark also praised Nori for his passing, kicking, and blocking.

The 150-pounder was the starting quarterback at DeKalb for four years. He also lettered in basketball, track, and wrestling (at 145 pounds). In his senior year in football he scored 113 points. He had one 35-point game, and in another game he returned a kick 102 yards for a touchdown. Nori, of Finnish descent, also won the "Little Nine" conference long jump title and ran a 9.9-second 100-yard dash in a meet against Loyola of Chicago.

When the Lions played the Dodgers at Ebbets Field in Brooklyn in 1937, Detroit won 30-0 against Clark's team, with the highlight being Vernon Huffman's pro record-setting 100-yard third-quarter interception return of a Nori pass for a touchdown.

WOBBLY ACCURACY

On the teams I was on, Eric Hipple threw some wobbly passes, and sometimes Chuck Long did, as well. Every now and then Greg Landry would let one loose that would go end over end. Gary Danielson and Bill Munson had the tightest spirals.

Long before them, the Lions most successful quarterback ever, Bobby Layne, was noted for throwing some "wounded ducks," too. Quarterbacks didn't necessarily have to have pretty passes to be successful, as Layne proved. Such was the case, too of former Michigan State star John Pingel, who briefly was with the Lions. He was accurate but "wobbly."

"They're the dog-gonedest looking passes I ever saw," assistant coach Bill Howard said in a story in *The Detroit News*. "They seem to float through the air aimlessly, but darned if they don't always seem to hit a receiver." Pingel graduated from high school when he was just 16. Between his freshman and sophomore years at MSU he spent a year at the U.S. Military Academy at West Point, but, according to Howard, couldn't hack the mathematics there.

10

DRAFT/FREE AGENT DEBACLES, SUCCESSES

MOTOWN LION?

There always are going to be "sleepers" in the draft, or free agent surprises, as well as local players who don't get selected by their own area teams, much to the consternation of local fans. And sometimes there are "candidates" who really have no chance at all—like when Motown singer Marvin Gaye wanted to try out with us. Marvin was a tremendous athlete and was in great shape. He was working out with Lem Barney, Mel Farr, and I and had the courage to go into camp.

Coach Joe Schmidt didn't think he was serious, but Marvin was, and when it cameright down to it, Joe backed out because Marvin was Mr. Motown at that time and he was afraid Marvin would get hurt and the Lions would be sued by Motown Records.

WONDERFUL WOJI

Andy Farkas was a big star at the University of Detroit in the mid-1930s, but although many felt the Detroit Lions might draft someone so good out of their own back yard in 1938, instead they went with hulking Fordham center Alex Wojciechowicz (C, LB, 1938-1946) as their No. 1 pick. When they signed him to a contract on the dotted line, joked *Windsor Star* sports columnist Vern Degeer, "In Wojie's case, two dotted lines were required."

Wojciechowicz was the 18th new player the team signed in 1938 as it embarked on a rebuilding campaign. Though some rough years were on the horizon, Wojie was a stalwart for nine years and in 1968 earned induction into the Pro Football Hall of Fame. (Farkas, by the way, did play for the Lions in 1945.)

Off-Hand Remark Lands Player

Someone who constantly interrupts is called a "but-insky," but the Lions wound up with their own "Batinsky" because someone else was a but-insky. The Lions were on the trail of a guard from the East in the summer of 1941 and found out he had signed with another team. But the player put his two cents worth in and asked aloud why Detroit had overlooked Stan Batinsky, a guard from Temple, who was a very good player who got no recognition. So on that advice alone the Lions sent Batinsky a letter asking him to report to camp and he wrote back saying he'd be there. He wound up having a solid nine-year NFL career, the first seven in Detroit. According to Lew Walter of the *Detroit Times*, Batinsky wore a size seven triple-E shoe "which gives him practically a square foot."

'O Sole Mio'

Some players in my time sought certain provisions in their contracts that, for instance, would guarantee them rooms for themselves on road trips. But I wasn't aware of any one as strange as the request from one player drafted three years before I was born. It was 1943 and because of World War II, good players who were certain not to be drafted had a little bit of bargaining power for a change. And some had special requests before they'd sign a contract. One of them was tackle Jack Irish, drafted from Arizona. He wanted the Lions to provide him with a singing instructor so he could study for an opera career.

Other Options

Every team has to contend with fans who gripe about who it chooses to draft. The Lions have drafted some real duds over the years in the early rounds, especially in the decades after their spectacular championships in the 1950s. But even in their heyday they didn't always guess right. Take their 1953 top draft pick, for instance. It was 230-pound tackle Dick Chapman of Rice. He decided to pass up pro football to devote his time to NUCLEAR PHYSICS. (Who said football players were dumb jocks?)

And their No. 2 pick that year, Michigan State center Jim Neal, married someone who was a member of a sect that frowned on sports on Sunday. Needless to say, Neal didn't pursue a pro football career.

Crossed Signals

There may not be many Lions fans who remember Detroit's second round draft pick in 1971, Dave Thompson (1971-1973), a center-guard from Clemson University. He became a backup lineman with the Lions for three years, but one year

10

DRAFT/FREE AGENT DEBACLES, SUCCESSES

MOTOWN LION?

There always are going to be "sleepers" in the draft, or free agent surprises, as well as local players who don't get selected by their own area teams, much to the consternation of local fans. And sometimes there are "candidates" who really have no chance at all—like when Motown singer Marvin Gaye wanted to try out with us. Marvin was a tremendous athlete and was in great shape. He was working out with Lem Barney, Mel Farr, and I and had the courage to go into camp.

Coach Joe Schmidt didn't think he was serious, but Marvin was, and when it cameright down to it, Joe backed out because Marvin was Mr. Motown at that time and he was afraid Marvin would get hurt and the Lions would be sued by Motown Records.

WONDERFUL WOJI

Andy Farkas was a big star at the University of Detroit in the mid-1930s, but although many felt the Detroit Lions might draft someone so good out of their own back yard in 1938, instead they went with hulking Fordham center Alex Wojciechowicz (C, LB, 1938-1946) as their No. 1 pick. When they signed him to a contract on the dotted line, joked *Windsor Star* sports columnist Vern Degeer, "In Wojie's case, two dotted lines were required."

Wojciechowicz was the 18th new player the team signed in 1938 as it embarked on a rebuilding campaign. Though some rough years were on the horizon, Wojie was a stalwart for nine years and in 1968 earned induction into the Pro Football Hall of Fame. (Farkas, by the way, did play for the Lions in 1945.)

Off-Hand Remark Lands Player

Someone who constantly interrupts is called a "but-insky," but the Lions wound up with their own "Batinsky" because someone else was a but-insky. The Lions were on the trail of a guard from the East in the summer of 1941 and found out he had signed with another team. But the player put his two cents worth in and asked aloud why Detroit had overlooked Stan Batinsky, a guard from Temple, who was a very good player who got no recognition. So on that advice alone the Lions sent Batinsky a letter asking him to report to camp and he wrote back saying he'd be there. He wound up having a solid nine-year NFL career, the first seven in Detroit. According to Lew Walter of the *Detroit Times*, Batinsky wore a size seven triple-E shoe "which gives him practically a square foot."

'O Sole Mio'

Some players in my time sought certain provisions in their contracts that, for instance, would guarantee them rooms for themselves on road trips. But I wasn't aware of any one as strange as the request from one player drafted three years before I was born. It was 1943 and because of World War II, good players who were certain not to be drafted had a little bit of bargaining power for a change. And some had special requests before they'd sign a contract. One of them was tackle Jack Irish, drafted from Arizona. He wanted the Lions to provide him with a singing instructor so he could study for an opera career.

Other Options

Every team has to contend with fans who gripe about who it chooses to draft. The Lions have drafted some real duds over the years in the early rounds, especially in the decades after their spectacular championships in the 1950s. But even in their heyday they didn't always guess right. Take their 1953 top draft pick, for instance. It was 230-pound tackle Dick Chapman of Rice. He decided to pass up pro football to devote his time to NUCLEAR PHYSICS. (Who said football players were dumb jocks?)

And their No. 2 pick that year, Michigan State center Jim Neal, married someone who was a member of a sect that frowned on sports on Sunday. Needless to say, Neal didn't pursue a pro football career.

Crossed Signals

There may not be many Lions fans who remember Detroit's second round draft pick in 1971, Dave Thompson (1971-1973), a center-guard from Clemson University. He became a backup lineman with the Lions for three years, but one year he was the long-snapper on punts and field goals and I was his backup. He was traded in January 1974 to New Orleans FOR THE SAINTS' NO. 1 DRAFT PICK. Why, one might ask, would a team squander its top draft choice for a backup offensive lineman? That's a good question, but apparently that's not what happened.

The Lions only THOUGHT they were trading Thompson straight up for the Saints' top pick. New Orleans, on the other hand, said the deal was that they would get Thompson AND DETROIT'S NO. 1 DRAFT CHOICE.

Needless to say, the Lions were embarrassed by the misinterpretation. After the Lions, picking in the Saints' eighth spot, selected Penn State linebacker Ed O'Neil, they prepared to take their own first-round choice at No. 13. Well, New Orleans said the Lions agreed to trade Thompson AND their No. 1 pick in order to move up to eighth in the draft, so the Saints took Ohio State linebacker Rick Middleton in Detroit's original spot.

"We had to let the draft proceed as it was," NFL Commissioner Pete Rozelle said. "There was no way of untangling it now."

Thompson's career ended after two years with the Saints. Middleton also played only two years with New Orleans and then three with San Diego before calling it quits. O'Neil, meanwhile, had a solid six-year career with Detroit through 1979 and led the team in tackles his last two seasons, ending his career in 1980 with Green Bay.

No one could be sure whom the Lions would have taken if they were able to select a draftee in the 13 spot, but reportedly they were interested in running back Woody Green of Arizona State. Green went three choices later to Kansas City and had a modest three-year career there. However, in Round Three the Lions did get a good running back, Dexter Bussey.

11

ECLECTIC EXECS

STRICTLY BUSINESS

Russ Thomas was strictly business. If there was a business I owned, he was the kind of guy I'd want to run it. There were sides to him people didn't understand and didn't know. The news media projected him to be one way and that was being tight with money and not spending a lot on players. They figured he just wanted to get by with the least product and essentially look at the club just as a business. But there was a human side to him that I got to know.

He was a caring man. One thing about Russ, if he liked you, he let you know. If he didn't like you, he'd let you know that, too, and you weren't going to change his mind. I learned a lot from him as a human being. He had a lot of smarts and wit about him, and people didn't give him credit for it because they thought he was just some hillbilly from Kentucky. But he was a very shrewd businessman.

I really missed him after he left the organization after the 1989 season. That was the beginning of my coaching career. Everybody respected him, but a lot of people were afraid of him. He was with the organization for 43 years and served in virtually every capacity, including time as a Lions broadcaster with Van Patrick. After Thomas died March 19, 1991, team owner William Clay Ford said: "Russ always had the best interests of his players at heart. He tried to look at the human side of each player and do what was best for that individual."

Chuck Schmidt, who succeeded Thomas as general manager, said Thomas's image "was all a style" and that "deep down he was much more sensitive than people would see. He had a very big tender side to him. Very few players ever found it, but when the did, they saw a different side of Russ Thomas." The Lions wore the initials "JRT" on their uniforms in 1991 to honor him.

INTERVIEW IN SLIPPERS

The person who handled the news media when the Lions started heading into their most glorious years of the 1950s was W. Nicholas Kerbawy, who I had the opportunity of meeting many years later. He didn't have a newspaper background but was a natural at publicity. He had been a schoolteacher in his native Blissfield, Michigan, for 11 years before becoming public relations director at Michigan State in 1944. That was when the Spartans restored the athletic program that had been halted with the advent of World War II.

Kerbawy was one of 72 applicants for the MSU job, according to *Detroit Skyliner*, a hotel magazine. He forgot to pack his shoes when he went to East Lansing for the interview and showed up wearing a suit—and slippers. Soon he was to become the nation's No. 1 collegiate sports publicist, as selected by the Helms Foundation of Los Angeles.

In 1948 the Hillsdale College graduate became PR director for the Lions, succeeding Fred Delano, and two years later also became assistant general manager when Lewis Cromwell became box office manager and treasurer at Olympia Stadium. In 1952 he took over as general manager as the Lions were headed into their zenith.

The team won NFL championships in 1952 and 1953, a Western division title in 1954, and another NFL crown in 1957. *Chicago Tribune* sports editor Arch Ward reported in 1955 that Kerbawy, as general manager, got a $10,000 bonus from Lions management for the job he did in 1954.

EXECS WELCOME

In a *Free Press* question-and-answer column from Mark Beltaire in 1960, GM Edwin Anderson said he asked coach George Wilson the previous season to take a private vote of players as to whether the directors could come into the locker room after games. The players said they could.

Nick Kerbawy rose from sports information director at Michigan State to become general manager of the Detroit Lions. *Photo courtesy of the Detroit Lions*

12

EMBARRASSING MOMENTS

Victoria's Secret

Probably my most embarrassing moment as a Lion—off the field—was the time I got pulled over by the police after a team Halloween party. It not only was embarrassing, it briefly was frightening. The party was at Larco's restaurant where we used to go after every home game. There were to be prizes for first, second, and third place. I decided to dress up in my wife's negligee and had Victoria's Secret underwear on and showed up at the party like that. I don't know if I took first, second, or third, but I won one of the prizes.

It was when we were headed home that I was stopped. I didn't have my license or any identification. I got out of the car and the policeman was looking at a six-foot-four woman with a negligee on. As soon as I got out I started telling him he wouldn't believe the story. He ended up laughing and letting me go because it could only have been the truth.

Pie Fun Goes Awry

Perhaps the most embarrassing team moment came in 1975, my eighth year in the league, during the annual "rookie show" at training camp at Oakland University. It got a little out of hand. The rookies were supposed to come up with some kind of award and they decided on a meringue pie for general manager Russ Thomas. Leonard Thompson was delegated to make the "presentation." He did so by smashing the pie jokingly into Russ's face—which didn't set too well with him. That was the last rookie show we ever had.

DE-PANTSED

But, hey, embarrassing moments weren't unique to my era. Guard Sam Knox (1934-1936), asked in August 1935 what his most embarrassing moment was, told *The Detroit News* that it was while he was a senior playing football for the University of Maine. He caught a pass in the flat and was running for a touchdown when, 20 yards from the goal line, the player trying to tackle him wound up holding Knox's pants "while I raced on."

"I grounded the ball behind the goal line," Knox said, "and kept right on running into the field house for another pair of pants."

OFF ON WRONG FOOT

Stillman Rouse sure didn't get off on the right foot when the 21-year-old rookie came into the Lions training camp in 1940 in hopes of making the team as an end. The 215-pounder from the University of Missouri, a boxing champion there, walked into the Lions offices on his first day and, according to E.A. Batchelor's account in *The Detroit News*, walked up to the man sitting at the desk, tickled him under the arm and said, "kitchy, kitchy, koo."

He, of course, had no way of knowing he had just tickled the team's new owner, Fred Mandel. Rouse didn't spend a lot of time in the Lions offices after that, and coach Potsy Clark instructed that before he addressed any veteran player he had to first salute and ask permission to speak.

Rouse had a penchant for ice cream sodas and soon gained 23 pounds. But he was a tough blocker, and Clark needed him fit and trim. By season's start he was down to 210 pounds. He played with the Lions only that one season.

SLEPT THROUGH IT

We picked up a fellow by the name of Rick Saul who also had a brother, Ron, in the league. Rick had a reputation for partying a lot. Different guys have different ways of getting themselves mentally ready to play. Some guys would read a book; some would lay out on the floor, close their eyes and meditate for a while. We had a game the day after Rick had been out partying and he was sleeping.

Coach Joe Schmidt was going around giving his pep talk. Some of the guys were still going through their meditation. It was time to get ready to go out for the kickoff and when we got out on the field and were looking for Rick, Schmidt sent one of the trainers to go see if he was inside. The trainer came back and said Saul was on the floor still asleep and asked the coach if he wanted him to go wake him up. Schmidt looked at him and said, "No, let him sleep, and when he wakes up tell him he's cut."

DON'T KILL THE HORSE

In my rookie year, 1968, we had an exhibition game in Kansas City. The Chiefs had a horse called "War Paint," and someone dressed as an Indian chief rode him up and down the sidelines, from one end zone to the other, every time the Chiefs scored a touchdown. And in that game they already had four or five touchdowns by halftime. Coach Joe Schmidt said in his halftime speech: "Guys, if we don't stop them from scoring, we will all go to jail for cruelty to animals.... You all are killing that damn horse."

13

FASHION PLATES?

PEER PRESSURE

Mel Farr, Lem Barney, and Greg Landry were the fashion setters of the Lions of the 1970s. Mel and Lem started a year ahead of Earl McCullouch, Greg and me. Earl and I didn't know much about fashion, but we got a quick education when Farr and Landry told us that until we went to Hot Sam's, where they bought the clothes everybody in Detroit wore and got ourselves three or four suits, we were not allowed to associate with them in public. That was the beginning of a change of fashion for Earl and me.

FRIENDLY PUTDOWN

Lions owner William Clay Ford used to have a blue blazer with a crest and gray slacks that he often wore on his visits to the locker room. If anyone was going to say anything about fashion, it was Lem Barney. He would joke with Mr. Ford, saying that he got his clothes at K-Mart. Mr. Ford would laugh his behind off.

He is a down-to-earth guy who happened to own Ford Motor Company. I loved to talk to his wife. She is very personable. I can remember William Clay Ford Jr. (who is now vice chairman of the franchise) wearing his little shorts and standing outside the locker room with Mrs. Ford and her daughter. Mrs. Ford always gave me a smile and a friendly hello. It is a beautiful family.

TAILOR-MADE?

One of the funniest stories, which, by the way, also involved my friend Earl McCullouch, happened on the night O.J. Simpson set the rushing record against us when Buffalo was at the Silverdome in 1976. He had 273 yards rushing, but we beat the Bills 27-14. Afterward, Simpson and McCullouch (who were teammates at Southern Cal) visited with us at our house.

O.J. started looking at my wedding album. Little did I know five years after the wedding that I had one pant leg of my tuxedo altered two or three inches shorter than the other one. O.J. actually got cramps in his side and tears in his eyes from laughter because every time he turned to another picture he saw the same thing, I had one pant leg longer than the other one. During the wedding, nobody told me about the problem.

That's the way I first met O.J. and we've been friends ever since, even through his murder trial ordeal. He's talked to me a couple times since. Every time I think of O.J. I think of that situation and have a lot of fun laughing about my wedding pictures.

IS THAT BING CROSBY?

Two generations earlier, Nick Kerbawy was Mr. Fashion Plate of the Lions. He "is a man you shouldn't miss seeing," Clotye Murdock, in the August 13, 1949, *Michigan Chronicle*, wrote of the Lions public relations man. "You can see him, in fact, a half mile away on a clear day in the country. It is then that Nick dons one of his favorite Bing Crosby-like outfits featuring lightweight cotton shirts in screaming colors, college-style hat and shoes.

"Nick's shirts are fascinating: Birds of Paradise flit on all their brightness across one of them; on another, a Hawaiian scene is pictured in shimmering sunset colors. He built up a gorgeous collection while he was athletic publicity director at Michigan State, [and] saves them for those times when he's out of the city." Murdock added that Kerbawy's country clothes "are not as bright as his personality."

14

FIFTH ESTATE

Death Takes Lions Writers

Various sports writers who have covered the Lions have died while still active in their craft, including in recent years Joe Falls and Joe Dowdall of *The Detroit News* and Jack Saylor of the *Free Press*. Sam Greene was sports editor of *The News* when he died August 5, 1963.

Perhaps the first Lions beat writer to die while an active reporter was Lloyd Northard of *The News*, who died in August 1936 at the age of 42 while the defending-champion Lions were in training camp for the new season. Northard was the victim of a cerebral hemorrhage, which struck while he was at his desk at *The News*. The World War I veteran had worked there 11 years. Pallbearers at his funeral in his hometown of Leslie, Michigan, were from the bowling community, with which he was most closely identified because of his coverage of that sport. He was an inaugural inductee into the Detroit Bowling Hall of Fame in 1958.

Plucked from the Papers

Lyall Smith was the sports editor of the *Free Press* when he was hired away in the late 1950s to become business manager and PR director of the team. I knew him as a nice, polite, smooth-talking man, which was the ideal personality for his position.

Although oft-times pro coaches and executives complain about the "poison pens" from the press, it wasn't unusual for them to pluck some of them from their newspapers and put them in the front office. The first time the Lions did that was in July 1938 when they named Manila Grant "Bud" Shaver as club vice president. Shaver was sports editor of the *Detroit Times* and had a 17-year career with the *Times*.

This Patton Was in Burma

While the Lions were losing players to World War II, so were newspapers losing sportswriters who covered the team. One of them was Harvey Patton of *The Detroit News*. The Lions news clip scrapbook from 1945 includes this item: "Harvey Patton is a civilian again and back on *The News* sports staff after serving in the Burma theater of war." Patton rose from private to captain and was awarded a Bronze Star medal. He was a star quarter-miler on the University of Michigan track team.

Keglers & Gridders

Bowling was one of our favorite pastimes to relax after a day at Lions training camp. There was a bowling center not far from our Cranbrook practice facility, and a bunch of us would go there. Some of the better bowlers were Mel Farr, Lem Barney, and Nick Eddy.

The Lions catered to bowlers when they played at Briggs Stadium. Through the efforts of Fred Wolf of WXYZ radio, they got their own section in the upper deck at the 30-yard line. "Each of the Lions home games are viewed by untold hundreds of bowlers," declared the *Modern Bowler* in February 1950. "Instead of being scattered all over Briggs Stadium, they will be in a friendly group."

The bowlers, and proprietors, got discounted tickets in the deal and the Lions got a rabid bunch of loyal fans. John N. Sabo, longtime *Free Press* sports writer who covered the Lions, left the paper to buy Grand Central Recreation, one of the nation's top bowling centers, and he also became president of the Bowling Proprietors Association of Michigan.

QB Club Banquets

The *Detroit Times* Downtown Quarterback Club held regular banquets and they generated lots of publicity. *The Times'* photo from the banquet of February 8, 1950, at the Masonic Temple featured coach Bo McMillin, draftee Leon Hart, and Jim Thorpe, who recently had been voted the top football player of the last 50 years. (Ten months later McMillin was fired.)

Patriarch Reminisces

Edgar Hayes was a native Detroiter who started writing sports in 1927, and when the Lions came to town he was one of the principal reporters covering them, while with the *Detroit Times*. He became sports editor there 1955 through 1960, when it was sold to *The News*. But he kept his skills honed in the late 1980s until his death writing a column for publisher Ron Cameron's *Sports Fans' Journal* magazine.

He was the patriarch of the town's sports writers then. He reminisced in his February 1987 column about his 65 years of following and covering sports. Here is some of what he said about the Lions: "When the Lions first came to Detroit, they blanked the first seven opponents. There haven't been seven shutouts in the league in the last five years." And, "Bobby Layne was hailed as the greatest football player the Lions ever had, but never in 15 years did he face Bronko Nagurski coming down the field like a runaway freight car, knowing he was supposed to do something about it. He never played one minute on defense."

Hayes, who for a time was the Michigan Racing Commissioner, wondered what the next 65 years would bring and said, "Lucky are those who will see them." In another column he said when the Lions first came to town some players were frequent visitors to Hayes's home.' "Like us, they were newlyweds and were stationed away from home the first time in their lives. They would often call Mrs. Hayes and offer to bring food if she would prepare dinner. They just wanted a home-cooked meal and the companionship and friendship of people like themselves. After dinner they would gather in the kitchen and clean up the place."

COLUMNIST ROBINSON

Will Robinson had a fabled basketball coaching career in Detroit and elsewhere, but in 1952 he was perhaps best known around town for his column, "Will Robinson's Sports Spotlight," in the *Detroit Courier*, circulated in the city's African-American community. His column December 6 that year was critical of the Lions' sale of Wally Triplett to the Cardinals. Triplett, Robinson told his readers, was "the only tan gridder under contract" with Detroit.

Robinson years later attended my wedding, which came after I signed with the Lions. The team sent him and Night Train Lane. I had a chance to sit down with them later and found both to be very interesting. Robinson was the kind of guy a black athlete could relate to. He could communicate with us. He is a very intelligent, smart man when it comes to athletics, and he can show you how to carry yourself in the community and advise you on things not to do. I respect him a lot.

BURGEONING ROLE OF PR

Among those who followed Fred Delano as PR representative were Bud Erickson, who was the team publicist for six years before being named assistant GM in 1958 when Edwin Anderson became general manager. Elliott Trumbull was the assistant PR person under Lyall Smith, being named to the position in July 1965 after having spent seven years as publicity director of the Red Wings.

The public relations department evolved immensely over the team's 70-plus year history, especially with the increase of TV coverage and advent of the Internet. Instead of one person and maybe an assistant, there now are a slew of department heads with secretaries, responsible for everything from press releases to marketing to community affairs to video production.

Heading it all up is Bill Keenist, senior vice president of communications and marketing, who steadily moved up from a general PR role over two decades with the Lions. Others include Matt Barnhart, the director of media relations, and Tim Pendell, senior director of community affairs.

'REST OF THE STORY'

An inspiration to Chuck Long, long before he was a quarterback for the Lions in the late 1980s and early 1990s, was his brother, Andy, who suffered from cerebral palsy. "I look at Andy and see he would give anything to be like me and it inspired me to work harder," Chuck Long said, during his days as a star quarterback (and Heisman Trophy runner-up) at Iowa.

A story about the brothers and their mutual respect and inspiration to each other was one of national radio commentator Paul Harvey's "The Rest of the Story" tales on ABC radio in 1986. Former Lions cornerback Lem Barney, now in the NFL Hall of Fame, shared the story in 1987 with readers of his column in *Sports Fans' Journal*.

'PASS'N THROUGH'

I wasn't quite sure where to put this item, but I guess it probably should go here with the writers (although I guess I fit into the Fifth Estate category since I was the Lions radio color commentator, 1983-1988, and radio broadcaster for the team in 1997).

During my playing days, the poetic muse hit me one day, and this is the result. On May 15, 1976, when I was near the end of my NFL playing career, I wrote this poem, called "NFL, Just Pass'n Through." I've got it framed now and on the wall in my office at the Lions' headquarters in Allen Park:

"Here today. Gone tomorrow.
"If you don't accept it, it's a life of sorrow.
"Trying to use our God-given talent.
"Being brave like the knight bold and gallant.
"Those who make it feel lucky indeed.
"It's God's own way of letting you succeed.
"Our efforts we extend in our hopes to win.
"Some play with their hearts, others just pretend.
"You give your all and nothing less.
"Today we win. Tomorrow we rest.
"You're not just a teammate, but my very best friend.
"Let's play together until the end.
"Today we'll hang together, just you and me.
"For tomorrow is a day we may never see."

15

FRUSTRATING RIVALRY

BEAT THOSE VIKINGS!

Coming out of the University of Minnesota, probably the hardest thing for me to overcome was not being able to beat the Vikings for five years. It was agony. I really felt the Vikings would draft me. They needed a tight end, but they passed on me, and that gave me added incentive against them. But the fact was we couldn't beat them for about five years. There were (and have been to this day) a lot of close games and last-minute losses.

I remember coach Rick Forzano telling us we couldn't have long sideburns and couldn't have beards. I don't think we could even have mustaches. We wanted to wear white shoes, and Forzano made us a deal—if we beat the Minnesota Vikings we could wear white shoes, as well as have beards and sideburns. Low and behold, we ended up beating them. Lem Barney intercepted a ball in the end zone on the last play to preserve the victory.

That was a terrible five years of trying. A lot of people said it was a jinx. We played over our head in that game we won. On the whole, we didn't match up with them talent-wise, but it always was a good series. From October 6, 1968, to September 22, 1974, we lost 13 consecutive games, the last being a 7-6 squeaker. The string ended when we beat them 20-16 on October 20, 1974. But September 26, 1976, we began a stretch of five more consecutive losses against Minnesota, and nine of 11.

16

GIFTED PLAYERS

Eleven Lions have been Heisman Trophy winners, emblematic of the top collegiate players in the nation, although that didn't always translate into pro stardom. Among the most gifted were Doak Walker and Leon Hart, mentioned in various places among these tales. But the Lions have had many other gifted players over the years, many during the frustrating title-less seasons from my era. And how could you not put Barry Sanders and Lem Barney at the top of that list?

WHO NEEDS BLOCKERS?

What can you say about Barry Sanders (RB, 1989-1998) that hasn't been said? He may be the best running back pro football ever has seen, and that's why he was inducted into the NFL Hall of Fame in 2004, his first year of eligibility. We'd watch game films of him, and you could see people flashing from one side to the other. When we'd slow the film down you could see that Barry was so far ahead of what was going on because he had anticipated his move prior to any action by the opponents.

Everyone defended us by trying to bring eight men in the box, and we knew we couldn't account for all of them from a blocking standpoint. We used to put the game plan together, and the offensive coordinator would say, "Well, who's got that eighth man?" And our answer would be that's Barry's man. He was such a tremendous athlete.

He actually ended up breaking the leg of Rod Woodson of Pittsburgh because of Woodson's reaction trying to cut back when Barry made a move on him with his great lateral quickness. If there was an unblocked man, Barry was probably the only man who played in the NFL who could essentially do his own blocking by simply making the guy miss.

A Sports Natural

Lem Barney (DB, 1967-1977) probably was the most gifted, talented athlete I've been around. The guy could do anything sports-wise, and he has a personality. People just love to be around him because he gives off such energy. As an athlete, they said the first time he ever picked up a set of golf clubs he shot scratch. He could bowl. He could play tennis. He could play basketball. He could do almost anything he wanted to do—and with the same grace. It was just as fluid as if he'd been doing it all his life.

My biggest thrill with him was being able to line up as a wide-out against him in practice, getting into a two-point stance, even though I was a tight end. I'd try to put the moves on this guy, when people who were 25, 30, 40 pounds lighter and a lot faster couldn't do it. Lem would just simply laugh the whole time the play was

The Lions in 2004 honored three of their greatest players by putting their Number 20 out of circulation, from left, Billy Sims, Lem Barney, and Barry Sanders.
Photo courtesy of the Detroit Lions

developing. He knew there was no way I was going to beat him. It was just a thrill to go out there and try.

He is a tremendous person and was tremendous athlete. I had a chance to room with him. We went through a lot together. To this day we're still friends and still talk to each other and laugh. He still has the same personality. He is just a joy to be around, and as a team we were spoiled because he was a guy who would make so many big plays from a defensive cornerback position. He'd get an interception, or a kickoff return, or a punt return, and run it in for a touchdown.

As the game went on and it was close, everybody pretty much figured Lem would save us, Lem would do something to put us in a position where we were going to win the ballgame. He just had that much talent. And being in the NFL Hall of Fame now is well-deserved. That is the greatest all-around athlete I'd say who's ever played for Detroit. He wore No. 20, as did two other greats, running backs Billy Sims and Barry Sanders. The Lions officially took that number out of circulation during a ceremony at the 2004 Thanksgiving Day game in honor of those players' achievements.

'MEL FARR, SUPERSTAR!'

Mel Farr (RB, 1967-1973) used his exceptional talent at football as a tool to help him in the business world. You could see he would be a businessman. He told me you have to learn to use football instead of it using you. It was a stepping-stone for the rest of your life, he would say, and I think that's the way he approached it. That led to him eventually getting his auto dealerships and the success in the business that he had.

When he suffered a critical knee injury he knew he didn't want to go through that type of pain and misery again, so after his first knee operation he retired from the Lions and became a successful businessman. When he left the game after seven seasons with Detroit he was among the franchise leaders in a number of categories. He was our offensive MVP in 1967 and 1968.

Was it any wonder his auto dealership TV commercials featured him in a Superman cape, with the slogan, "Mel Farr, superstar."

POTENTIAL REACHED ELSEWHERE

Ron Jessie (WR, 1971-1974) was the fastest man on the team. He probably had more talent than anybody realized, and it showed up later when he went to the Los Angeles Rams. He never really was used the way he should have been by the Lions, which was evident when he went to L.A. and had a great career out there.

Mel Farr wore a superhero cape during his TV car dealership commercials.
Photo courtesy of the Detroit Lions

CAT-QUICK

Jerry Ball (NT, 1987-1992) was one of the first 325-pounders the Lions had. He was only six foot one, so with his weight he looked like a human bowling ball. Yet the rotund nose tackle was quick as a cat. If you looked at him you would think he couldn't move in a straight line and didn't have the speed that he did. We on the staff made a lot of money off Ball by betting anyone on the team that within the first 15-20 yards he could beat anyone in a race. Sure enough, we had guys like Mel Gray and Barry Sanders willing to take that bet on.

In the majority of cases, Jerry Ball won the race, though after his first spurt he started to peter out. But in the first 15-20 yards, Jerry Ball probably was the fastest guy on the team. So what happened in the Gray-Sanders-Ball race? Coach Wayne Fontes was the judge and he called it a tie. But I said Jerry won because more of his stomach was over the finish line.

RECEIVING IS A GRAY AREA

Mel Gray (KR/WR, 1989-1994) was one of the most feared kick returners in the history of the NFL, and for three consecutive years with us (1991-1993) he was named to the Pro Bowl at the position. Although he also was listed as a wide receiver, our run-and-shoot offense was so complicated it was difficult for him to master both responsibilities, and so we had to give him more simplified receiving plays. I was in the first year of my eight-year coaching stint with the Lions when Mel joined the team in 1989. I coached tight ends from 1989-1990, then wide receivers from 1991-1996.

Coach Wayne Fontes kept preaching about Gray's speed, and so we had to get him in as a wide-out because he would be so tough to cover. So after some arm twisting we finally got him in a game as a starter. The very first play I called was a pass play, and the quarterback dropped back and hit Gray for a first down. We called another play and, boom, first-down completion to Mel.

That happened three times in a row, and all of a sudden you could hear Wayne call upstairs to the booth and he said, "Charlie, I told you he could play, I told you he could play." I called him back and said, "Wayne, we called three pass plays in a row and he ran three wrong routes in a row." Wayne said not to worry and he'd tell the quarterback just to keep an eye on him and follow him, and when he stopped, throw the ball to him. We kept him in the game for almost a quarter and never threw it to him again. Wayne came to us and said, "I think we pushed our luck enough, get him out."

Blind No. 1 Draft Pick?

Herman Moore (WR, 1991-2001) was one of my favorites, and I had the opportunity to coach him. When Herman came out of the University of Virginia he was our No. 1 draft choice, an All-American. One time we were running the run-and-shoot offense, which basically consisted of, as I called them, "midgets," guys who were about five foot eight at wide receiver. But Herman was tall (6-4).

I remember in the 1991 preseason we were in the midst of installing the run-and-shoot, and by the time preseason was over a couple things had happened—No. 1 was that Herman Moore wasn't having the best rookie start. He was dropping a lot of balls and no one knew why. Coach Wayne Fontes came to me and said, "Every time I look up, I see these midgets on the field and it's kind of a problem. We've got this 6-4 athlete we drafted on the first round, and I'm wondering what the problem is." My answer was that he wasn't ready yet.

We decided to get his eyes checked, and basically found out Herman couldn't see. We didn't know he wore contacts in college, but he decided for whatever reason he wouldn't wear them in the pros. When we checked his eyes we did indeed find out he was almost blind out on the field. Herman went on to become the best wide receiver in the history of the Detroit Lions.

Moore was unique in that he always wanted to know the answer to why we were doing things. I once asked him if his coach ever got tired of his B.S. in college and kicked him out. He wanted to know the why of everything, he said, for the betterment of his game in the pros, and the only way that could happen was to have the answers.

First Lions Superstar

In our lobby in Allen Park there's a huge photo mural and it depicts many of the great Lions over the years. Today's fans would recognize a lot of them, but there were others from previous eras who were every bit the football legends that the likes of Barry Sanders, Lem Barney, and others were. Among them was Earl 'Dutch' Clark (B, 1934-1938), who was a superstar not just in Detroit, but throughout the country. He could be seen on the covers of countless magazines. The *Detroit Times* promoted an upcoming issue that would feature a color shot of Clark in the Sunday gravure section, "suitable to frame" and his image was plastered on countless other such covers.

He wrote columns in newspapers and magazines. One of his magazine columns ran in *Young America*, a national news weekly for youth. If he wasn't writing something himself, someone else was making him the feature of a huge article. *Collier's* magazine, which cost five cents, highlighted a Clark feature on the cover of one of its issues in 1937.

Earl "Dutch" Clark was the big headline maker for the earliest Lions teams, deservedly so because he was a superstar. *Photo courtesy of the Detroit Lions*

Now & Then, a pictorial magazine, ran a story in November 1937 comparing Clark and the legendary Jim Thorpe. It gave the edge to Clark as the greatest football player of all time. It used a table of 100 points each for various categories, and Clark came out on top overall, 605-570. Clark had the edge in punting (85-80), passing (75-65), drop kicking (90-80), defense (90-85), and field generalship (95-85). They were tied in running at 90 points each, while Thorpe won out in blocking, 85-80.

"It's 1937 and the records of yesteryear have long since been forgotten in the light of feats of the young men who have come to the fore since that time," wrote *Chicago Daily News* columnist Ed Bang, tempering the article's findings.

In one of the syndicated columns of legendary sports writer Grantland Rice, he interviewed Bob Zuppke, the famed Illinois player and coach, and reported on his assessment of the greatest players in pro football in 1937 and Clark was one of the top four quarterbacks. Zuppke said he wouldn't want to pick just one because it would be slighting other greats, so he picked four for every backfield position. One of the players he picked at right halfback was Frank Christensen of the Lions and another was former Lion Father Lumpkin of the Dodgers. Ernie Caddell was one of Zuppke's picks at left halfback, and at fullback, Ace Gutowsky was one of the four best.

There was a "Dutch Clark Day" at the Thanksgiving Day game at UD in 1937 (the Lions beat the Bears 13-0). Kids wrote poems, and players wrote tributes for the program. And… Clark was given a new car! With all Clark's accomplishments, for some reason Lions principal owner Dick Richards saw fit to supply him with his own personal press agent, Steve Hannagen, noted as the voice of the Indianapolis Speedway, Arlington Park Race Track outside Chicago, and as PR man for the city of Miami Beach.

"Yet, without distracting from Hannagen's genius, Clark's best press agent still is, as it has always been, Clark himself," wrote Howard Roberts of the *Chicago Daily News*, alluding to his great ability.

"A quiet, studious-appearing fellow off the field, Clark looks nothing at all like the typical football hero. The glasses he wears off the field make him look too meek. And he seems too small." Clark, at 178 pounds, was the lightest guy on the team.

News stories variously reported him as being of English or Danish decent, certainly not Dutch. Roberts said Clark got his nickname in a rather unusual way: His eldest brother developed a dialect that hinted at a Dutch accent, so his family started calling him "Big Dutch." When another Clark baby boy arrived, he soon was called, "Little Dutch." So when Earl arrived as the third brother, he was just "Dutch."

Although it isn't often mentioned, Clark had another nickname, "Queenie."

THIS GUY WAS A WHIZ

The United States was on the cusp of becoming a participant in World War II when Byron "Whizzer" White was starring in the Lions backfield. In fact, when he

Gifted Players

signed August 14, 1940, with Detroit, the banner headline of the signing (in somewhat smaller type) ran above *The Detroit News*' front page headline that declared: "Nazis Launch 'Total Blockade.'"

White, a six-foot-one, 190-pounder from the University of Colorado, made his NFL debut in 1938 with the Pittsburgh Pirates, who reportedly paid him the then-whopping sum of $15,000. He sat out the 1939 season and went to England on a Rhodes scholarship. World War II, though, forced him to return home, and subsequently the Lions signed him.

"The reason I turned to football is because I love to play it," *The News* article quoted him as saying. "I have always heard about Detroit ever since Dutch Clark came here a few years ago and made good in the pro game."

Pittsburgh agreed to release the triple-threat ace, the most highly publicized player since Red Grange, from his contract in exchange for compensation from the Lions—who later would lose him, like so many others, to the military.

17

INJURY SETBACKS AND MEDICAL ODDITIES

GOOD HANDS?

People may have said Charlie Sanders had good hands as a receiver with the Lions. But in college I had horrible hands, at least for my first two years. In fact, I had a ligament ripped in my left thumb, an injury I suffered in high school while playing defensive end. I never got it fixed until my junior year in college. I can still pull the thumb backwards.

I went to Minnesota as a 185-pound flanker. But I had a problem holding on to balls in my freshman season. I would tape my thumb to my index finger. No one paid much attention to that, they just thought I couldn't catch. In my sophomore year they moved me to defensive safety. By then I was up to 200 pounds and didn't have to catch the ball.

I didn't see much playing time those first two years. Then, after my sophomore year, they decided to take a look at my thumb and discovered the torn ligaments. The ligaments were reattached. The Kansas City Chiefs drafted Aaron Brown, our All-America tight end and defensive end, and I was moved to defensive end after putting on about 30 pounds.

It was in my senior year that I was switched to tight end, since our starter had left. That ligament operation I had must have worked, because suddenly people were saying things like, "I didn't know you could catch."

I guess the rest is history.

GESTURE OF RESPECT

Ben Davis had a potentially brilliant career at Cleveland, only to have injuries mar it. We got him in a trade as an extra defensive back. One thing about him that stood out was his perfect Afro, and I patterned mine after his.

A broken thumb during his playing days at the University of Minnesota didn't help Charlie Sanders, but in his days with the Lions he was noted for his good hands as a receiver. The reason he's kicking up water here is that there was a leak in the Silverdome roof. *Photos courtesy of the Detroit Lions*

If anyone deserved a game ball after the Lions beat his old Browns team 21-10 November 9, 1975, at Pontiac Stadium (which wasn't yet called the Silverdome) it was Davis (1974-76). He was healthy and playing in place of injured superstar cornerback Lem Barney, an eventual NFL Hall of Famer. Davis returned an interception 67 yards for a fourth-quarter touchdown that broke the back of the Browns—who had traded him to Detroit in 1974 after seven seasons in Cleveland.

But what did Davis do after getting the game ball? He gave it to Barney, who was heartsick at not being able to play because of a bruised thigh.

"Barney is THE left cornerback of the Detroit Lions," Davis said.

Cleveland picked Davis in the 17th round of the draft in 1967. He played all 14 games, had one interception, and led the league in punt returns. Then he really blossomed the next season, intercepting eight passes and returning them for 162 yards. However, he missed the entire 1969 season due to two knee operations. The Birmingham, Alabama, native wasn't the same after that, yet was still a capable defensive back, pulling in eight interceptions in his last five years with the Browns.

Detroit got the Defiance (Ohio) College star in exchange for a fifth-round draft choice. He started three games at right cornerback for Detroit that year, then ran into more tough luck in 1975, undergoing an operation for a fractured thumb (suffered in the first preseason game) and one for a fractured wrist (November 16, a week after the Browns game).

Betrayed By Knees

Steve Owens (1970-1975) wasn't the most gifted running back, even though he won the Heisman Trophy and many other accolades at Oklahoma. But he was a tough kid and earned the respect of the Lions. When we went to Miami and were getting killed and couldn't score, he was determined to score. He took the ball on every play of the last series. It was hot, and the Dolphins knew Owens was going to get the ball and they were pounding him. Needless to say, Steve carried all 20 plays of a 20-play drive that showed how tough he was.

It was a shame he suffered his knee injury at a time when he was just coming into his own. I can recall the day he was going for the goal line when he got popped on his knee. That was the end of his career. It was a tremendous loss to us.

It was the same type of situation with Lawrence Gaines (1976-1979). He was a big, burly fullback who we called "Big House". He was one heck of a powerful running back who also was just coming into his own when a knee operation ended his career in 1979 after four years with Detroit.

Sock Lock

NFL football players take a lot of pounding and suffer a lot of injuries, but as a result of putting on your socks? Our center for a couple years, Larry Tearry (1978-1979), a rookie from Wake Forest, nearly missed the Thanksgiving Day game in

Injury Setbacks and Medical Oddities

1978 because he was briefly incapacitated while putting on his socks—somehow his knees locked. "It took 40 minutes of work by our doctors to unloosen things so he could play," coach Monte Clark said. His knee clicked into place just three minutes before game time.

Tearry, a fourth-round draft pick, came to camp in bad shape but worked himself into condition and became the starting center the last 12 games. After the season he underwent knee surgery to repair the trick knee problem that bothered him several times. The former All-Atlantic Coast Conference player was with the Lions for just two years and then was out of the NFL.

RIGHT SIDE IS WRONG SIDE

Knee and foot injuries go with the territory, but in the Lions' first year in the league they had a guard, Ray Richards, who had something no one else had. When he was playing football at the University of Nebraska, physicians there had to remove his appendix. Imagine their surprise when they found that his heart was on the right side of his body instead of the left like everyone else. Besides football, Richards wrestled. In fact, wrestling for noted promoter Nick Londes, he won three-fourths of all his matches and during one two-year span he went without a loss.

18

INNOVATORS AND INNOVATIONS

Pioneer Protective Gear

Mel Farr was the first running back I saw who wore a flak jacket to protect his ribs. Some of our quarterbacks did, also. Who would have known that the idea probably started at Stanford University many decades earlier—and to benefit halfback Ernie Caddel, who was one of the cornerstones of the Lions first team in 1934. Leo Macdonell, writing in the September 21, 1934, *Detroit Times*, said Caddel suffered two broken ribs while playing for Stanford against Oregon State, and his coach, Pop Warner, made him an aluminum vest to protect his ribs.

"Pop made a paper pattern one day and the thing that night," Macdonell quoted Caddel as saying. "It was an ingenious affair.... It had steel ribs, but you hardly noticed the weight."

Toe Tactics

My friend Errol Mann, the outstanding kicker, would file the toe of the shoe on his kicking foot. It was the strangest thing. And Wayne Walker, our great linebacker and kicker before Mann, had a squared-off toe that he'd attach to his shoe, tied in the back. He probably didn't realize it, but the device may have originated with one of the greatest Lions from their early years, Dutch Clark.

He was the last drop-kicker in the NFL, but he finally decided during training camp of 1938 to try placekicking the ball for conversions and field goals, although his dropkicking prowess helped him lead the league in scoring five of the previous six seasons.

Clark said an ingrown toenail on his right foot helped convince him to make the switch, and he began using a square-toed hard rubber toe that slipped over a shoe.

He said the toe device weighed just a half-pound, "but it seems to weigh three pounds on your foot."

DOMED STADIUM

When we played at Tiger Stadium I don't think we envisioned moving out of the city to play in a new domed stadium. But while looking through our old scrapbooks I found out that long before the Silverdome was built in Pontiac, the Lions were thinking about one.

During the turmoil by new Lions owner Fred Mandel in 1940 on whether the team would be allowed to use Briggs Stadium, he announced, through vice president Tony Owen, that he would expand UD Stadium by about 7,000 seats to 27,000. "We intend to build, either by ourselves or in conjunction with the University of Detroit, a football stadium which will be adequate for big league football in Detroit for years to come," Owen told *Toledo Blade* sports columnist Bob French. "I might go a bit further and say that we are even considering plans for a stadium which ultimately can be enclosed so that games can be played at night or in any sort of weather.

"Costs in major league football are increasing rapidly and it may be, when the clubs are carrying about 45 men each, that two games a week will be played, both to increase the income and to satisfy the demands of the public. That may mean night games indoors."

That talk might have been a ruse to extract a deal from Walter Briggs, but the ideas were visionary. The Lions ended up moving to a domed stadium in Pontiac 35 years later, night games became common to accommodate TV, and rosters grew to beyond 45 players. Teams didn't play two games a week, but fans' love for football was quenched with countless TV games from the networks and with the advent of cable and satellite TV.

NEW NUMBERING SYSTEM

I wore No. 88, but had it not been for an old Lions coach, maybe I'd have had some odd number you'd never see today on a receiver. Credit can go to 1941 Lions coach William Edwards for instituting a new numbering system for players, which he said would help the fans watching the games. All wingbacks would be numbered 10-19; blocking backs 20-29; fullbacks 30-39; tailbacks 40-49; centers 50-59; guards 60-69; tackles 70-79; ends 80-89. Detroit was the first team in the league to introduce the system. "Football should be played for the fans," Edwards said, in a *Detroit Times* article in July that year. "After all, it's the fan who spends his money to see the game…" A similar system was later implemented league-wide and still is utilized today.

Receivers Gloves

I wasn't one for wearing gloves in a game, but if I had the off-season occupation of Dave Diehl, I'd probably wear them at work. Diehl, of Michigan State, played for Detroit in 1939-1940 and 1944-1945. He wore doeskin gloves while working on his farm near Dansville, Michigan. "If I didn't wear them, my hands would get hard and calloused and I'd have trouble catching passes," he said, in a *Free Press* story by Dale Stafford. What might he think if he knew that 30 years later receivers all over the league would be wearing special gloves—in games?

No Passing Fancy

Passing was long a mainstay in the NFL game when Gus Dorais was the Lions coach in the 1940s, but occasionally newspaper columnists had to remind readers that Dorais was one of the pioneers who made that element of the game a staple. One column by George Carens in an unidentified newspaper clip from November 1945 told of the "Game that changed football history" on November 1, 1913. That was when Notre Dame, a tiny, obscure Catholic university from South Bend, Indiana, upset the Cadets from West Point 35-13 thanks to the seldom-used forward pass.

It was Dorais, the Fighting Irish back from Chippewa Falls, Kansas, who threw the passes to the team captain, a guy named Knute Rockne, for that historic triumph, completing 14 of 17 passes. When the Irish returned home, Dorais stayed behind at Army's request to help teach the cadets the passing game. Even more obscure for Lions fans was that before the shocking victory over Army, the Dorais-Rockne combo was unleashed at South Bend in a 62-0 crushing of Alma College of Michigan.

The two future famous gridiron legends had decided to try the pass connections after tossing the ball around on the beaches at Cedar Pointe Amusement Park on Lake Erie in Ohio when they were there working as lifeguards the previous summer.

Low Cuts

We were required to wear black shoes, but they could be low cuts. I, though, wore high tops because of problems with my ankles. Our quarterback, Greg Landry, also wore high tops.

As it turns out, the Lions may have been in the first game involving a pro team in which low cuts were worn. They were playing against the Army All-Stars in September 1942 to raise money for Army Emergency Relief. The Army players were wearing low cut shoes. Army coach Wallace Wade had his players wear light baseball shoes with football cleats and players taped their ankles. The heavier-footed, high-topped Lions, playing before a crowd of 21,499 (including 1,200 standing room) at UD Stadium, lost 12-0. But the game raised $30,492.

Platoon System

It was difficult enough to play tight end in the NFL, especially against some of those often-angry defensive players like Dick Butkus, but how did they ever play both offense and defense in the NFL and survive for very long?

Maybe today we should thank coach Bo McMillin of the Lions for changing that. McMillin's 1950 team arrived at training camp in Ypsilanti in August 1950, and Edwin J. Anderson, one of the new principal owners, along with D. Lyle Fife, said the group was "the best the Lions ever assembled for training—at least it's the best on paper." The team had an exhibition game in Birmingham, Alabama, and the *Birmingham News* wrote of McMillin: "Not two teams does he use, not three or four, but seven. He calls his system the 'multi-platoon system'. He used a team to kick off, a different team to receive a punt. Then Bo has his offensive team and defensive team and a very important unit—a point-after-touchdown team."

Unfortunately, those innovations didn't help McMillin. After winning three of their first four games, the Lions lost four in a row, and soon people were crying for his head. Fritz Crisler of the University of Michigan was wanted for the job, one newspaper speculated. McMillin got the axe December 19.

Two-Minute Drill

The day after McMillin was fired, the 37-year-old Buddy Parker replaced him at a reported salary of $12,000. Parker would go on to introduce the two-minute offense. He was the first to design an offense for the closing minutes of a game, and the Lions worked on it daily. Who doesn't like to watch a quarterback today deftly handle a team in the last two minutes of a half?

Radio Helmets

With all the satellite communications these days, there would be all kinds of opportunities for coaches to communicate with players on the field, if it was legal. A half-century ago, the Lions tried out a radio system for their October 14, 1956 game against the Rams—with my old coach, then the star linebacker, Joe Schmidt receiving signals in his helmet from assistant coach Buster Ramsey.

"I'm sure it will facilitate defensive signals," coach Buddy Parker said, in *The Detroit News* story by Buck Rogers.

"I'm for it solidly," Schmidt said. "We can always use a 12th man."

Ramsay would relay coded formations from the bench based on the observations he and assistant Aldo Forte made from the sidelines and Red Cochran from the press box. GM Nick Kerbawy said the club paid $450-$600 for the electronics, including $42 for a field microphone, $300 for 2,200 feet of wire, $150 for field amplifiers, $79.50 for the receiver, and $290 for labor.

Commissioner Bert Bell told the *Free Press*, meanwhile, that the innovation was OK with him, "but I hope nobody starts wiretapping." And in an AP story he said: "There is nothing in the rules now to prevent the use of such equipment."

A week later, Bell issued an edict outlawing the gadget, used by the Lions and Cleveland Browns, after a majority of owners said they were opposed to it.

After the October 14 game, Schmidt said: "I caught myself looking around a couple times to see what he [Ramsey] was doing out on the field."

HALL SITE

I'd certainly like to be inducted into the Pro Football Hall of Fame in Canton, Ohio, one of these days, but sometimes I wonder about what it takes to get in. Sometimes if you're not from a big-market city like New York or Los Angeles, or teams that get a lot of national TV exposure—or win championships—the prospects aren't as bright. I wonder if it would have made any difference if the NFL Hall of Fame happened to be in Detroit—something that was a possibility at one time.

In the summer of 1959, president Edwin Anderson of the Lions headed a committee to look into establishing such a shrine in Detroit.

METAL CLEATS

At training camp in 1960, the Lions started wearing the newly approved metal-tipped cleats instead of rubber. *The News* ran a photo of equipment manager Friday Macklem with the shoes. The story explained that metal cleats sometimes developed a razor-sharp edge. Gil Mains got a four-stitch cut over an eye when halfback Terry Barr accidentally kicked him with his flying metal cleats in practice.

MILDEW PROOF

Friday Macklem was our equipment manager throughout my years as a player. I had no idea that, in the 1960 season, he invented an equipment bag with air vents to prevent mildew. He called it the "Air Sack" and said the University of Minnesota was using it on its trip to the Rose Bowl game. Also, Macklem said, "I'm working on a practice blocking shield which will be light and more durable than anything on the market."

Electrical Stimulation

Trainer Kent Falb hooked me up once with what we called a TNS unit, a device to stimulate your muscles, which wasn't legal. Trainer Kent Falb cut a hole in the back of my shoulder pads and put in the wallet-sized unit, with two wires running down to my hamstring muscles in the back of my legs. There were two knobs to increase or decrease the electrical stimulation. It was something like putting your finger in a socket and getting a jolt. It was considered similar to getting an injection. It took your mind off the pain.

The knobs were in the back and I couldn't reach them. Once I asked Dan Jaroshewich, Friday Macklem's assistant equipment manager, to turn them on for me. He turned them too high, and I just took off running, and he ran after me to try to turn them down.

Longtime Lions trainer Friday Macklem, shown here passing out equipment in 1945, invented an equipment bag with air vents to prevent mildew.
Photo courtesy of the Detroit Lions

Taped Practices

We used to have three or four cameras for filming our games and we could study the film. But it was three years before I came to the Lions, July 1966, that the team began videotaping practices. The Lions paid $11,000 for the tape equipment, Jim Taylor of the *Toledo Blade* reported. Said coach Harry Gilmer, "It will tend to eliminate bad habits before they can take hold."

No Knee-Jerk Reaction

Our equipment managers often would try to design something to protect an injury, but Jack Johnson, a Lions tackle from 1934 to 1940, worked on something himself when he couldn't find decent protection for his knees. He invented a hinged knee guard. The story, by E.A. Batchelor Jr. of *The Detroit News* in November 1938, said the invention evolved with the help of Dave Brady, a mechanically inclined friend of Johnson. Players Bill Feldhaus and Sid Wagner converted to the new knee guard, and a couple other players said they would be interested. During the off-season Johnson started producing the guards at his ranch home in Grantsville, Utah. He was a one-man assembly line.

Territorial Draft

At the NFL's annual owners' meeting in 1940, the Lions proposed that the upcoming April 6 draft would include a territorial provision. It would allow for a team to get first choice over any college player within a 150-mile radius. The hope was that Detroit would get to pick University of Michigan great halfback Tom Harmon. But the suggestions fell on deaf ears. A couple decades later, the upstart American Football League installed a territorial provision.

19

KNUCKLE SANDWICHES

Many Lions over the decades were involved in fights, either on the field or off. Barroom scuffles often made headlines, and there were plenty of noteworthy events besides the much-publicized Alex Karras-Dick the Bruiser affair and their subsequent for-profit wrestling match. I'd heard of some of the more notable ones, but I don't know of many serious ones involving my teammates. Our coach, Joe Schmidt, kept a close watch on that kind of behavior.

END ENDS LIONS SERVICE

There was one incident when Joe Robb (DE, 1968-1971) and Bill Malinchak (E, 1966-1969) got in a fight at a bar and Malinchak wound up being traded to Washington. Only a few people knew what happened. In a meeting the next day, Joe was wearing dark glasses. He was beat up and bruised. We called him "Whiskey Joe." Anyway, the story I got was that he swung at Malinchak and fell, and, like any smart receiver would do, Malinchak wouldn't let him get up.

That altercation didn't have near the excitement or headline power of some of the confrontations from the Lions glory days, such as the ones Bob "Hunchy" Hoernschemeyer and Bob Smith got involved in.

HUNCHY BELTS COP

The headline in the July 23, 1954, *Detroit Times* read: "Lions Ace Pleads Guilty in Dawn Café Brawl." The ace was running back Bob "Hunchy" Hoernschemeyer, who lost a tooth scuffling with two former Ann Arbor High School players in Ann Arbor. The two apparently started the brawl, and all three involved pled guilty before Municipal Judge Francis O'Brien and were released on $25 bail.

Lions receiver Dorne Dibble was with Hoernschemeyer and an attractive young woman when the two guys made a crack about her and were told to shut up. One of the young men swung at Hoernschemeyer, who swung back and, according to the newspaper article, "accidentally belted a policeman" who was one of two who intervened at the White Spot restaurant on Main Street. The Lions had been quartered at a dormitory at Michigan Normal College (Eastern Michigan) nearby for training camp.

SF SCRAP

Hoernschemeyer and halfback "Tulsa Bob" Smith were involved in a fight in San Francisco in October 1953, getting into it with two loudmouths at a restaurant who they asked to step outside. They did, and one of the men swung at Smith and was flattened by a counter punch. Hoernschemeyer then grabbed the other guy by the seat of his pants and tossed him over a stone wall. (The Lions beat the 49ers 14-10.)

Two of the principals involved in a fight in San Francisco outside a restaurant were Bob "Hunchy" Hoernschemeyer, left, and "Tulsa Bob" Smith, who is standing here behind quarterback Bobby Layne (22), who just took a practice snap from Laverne Torgeson. That's Doak Walker next to Layne. *Photo courtesy of the Detroit Lions*

L.A. Scrap

Smith was going to retire after the 1953 season but was persuaded to go another year—only to run into more hot water November 1, 1954, in an incident that ended his career. Players always have complained about not getting enough playing time, but Smith got a bit too upset about that on a charter flight preparing to take off from Los Angeles after the Lions' 27-24 victory over the Rams. There was a sharp exchange of words between Smith and assistant coach Gerard "Buster" Ramsey, and they started scuffling.

According to the story in the *Times*, coach Buddy Parker immediately kicked Smith off the team—and off the plane—but relented and let him back on the flight. The next day Smith was released on waivers. The fight was broken up before any real punches were landed.

Sam Greene, writing in *The News*, said Hoernschemeyer, Doak Walker, Les Bingaman, and co-captains Thurman McGraw and Laverne Torgeson, lobbied to keep Smith on the team, to no avail. Smith, who was in his sixth season, said he would go back to his job at Ford Motor Company. Lyall Smith of the *Free Press* later wrote that Smith deserved a better fate.

'Mains' Events

The first time the team made headlines in 1962 was because of a fight in January in which "four or five" men beat up Gil Mains and Howie Young of hockey's Red Wings on a Saturday night at the Intermission Room bar at the Jefferson Hall Hotel. Mains said he and Young suffered multiple minor injuries.

Whatever started it, one of the guys put his hands on Mains and said, "Do you want to make something out of it?" and the guy tried to hit him and Mains pushed him away. Before long the others joined in. Mains ended up reporting the incident to the 1st Police Precinct. Since it was during the hockey season, the Red Wings sent perennial bad boy Young down to its Edmonton farm club for a few days under suspension for drinking.

Although it can't be considered a fight in the barroom brawl sense, Mains was involved in another incident in which he was the hero. He was returning home after midnight in the off-season of 1960 from his job as an insurance salesman, saw two youths siphoning gas from a neighbor's car in Fraser. The six-foot-three, 250-pounder chased them over a fence, tackled them, and put a wrestling hold on them. They both were 20-year-olds, one from Roseville and the other from Mount Clemens.

NEEDLING FOR EFFECT

It wasn't a fight, as such, but Craig Hertwig (OT, 1975-1977) got into it at one practice with Marv Hubbard (FB, 1977), who was only making an effort to toughen him up. Hertwig was a big tackle from Macon, Georgia, and an All-American from the University of Georgia. He was six foot eight, 285 pounds, and had all the physical attributes you'd want in a tackle when he was drafted on the fourth round in 1975.

In 1977 we acquired Hubbard from the Oakland Raiders. He was a member of their championship team and was the kind of player the Lions needed. After about a week, Hubbard noticed Hertwig was a little soft in his play, and he was getting on him because Hertwig had the physical attributes but just didn't want to put them to good use.

Hubbard kept needling Hertwig and an argument developed. Hubbard basically told him he had to get mean and want to hurt people and things like that. It went on for a few minutes and out of nowhere you hear this big pop, flesh meeting flesh. It was Hertwig's fist meeting Hubbard's cheek and we thought there were going to be big fisticuffs. But Hubbard just backed up and said, "Now that's what I'm talking about! If you can do that to me, just think what you can do to somebody you don't like."

Another thing about Hertwig, his main objective for playing in the NFL, he said, was to own a 7-11 store with a pool table in it. I don't think that ever happened.

THIS FIGHT COUNTS

There was one fight that made me especially proud and it didn't involve me, any teammates, or any bar rooms. It was the International Boxing Association's Continental junior-welterweight WOMEN'S boxing championship in Sault Ste. Marie, Michigan, in the fall of 2004. That's when my daughter, Mary Jo Sanders, won a 10-round unanimous decision over Chevelle Hallback. That improved Mary Jo's record to 9-0 in 15 months of boxing.

Mary Jo probably could have done just about anything she wanted to do. She wasn't the most gifted athlete, but she had that temperament. She started out bodybuilding. I said OK, I can live with that. Then she wanted to get into some kind of aerobics that were a little different, so she got into kickboxing and tied that into aerobics. The next thing you know, she's in the ring kickboxing, and then from there she's fighting Toughwomen contests. She won those three years in a row here and the national title, which included some prize money, and so then she had to turn pro.

It was hard enough to watch that one. I've been wearing the same sweater to every fight since. When she won the belt, I put on a different sweater, but I took the other

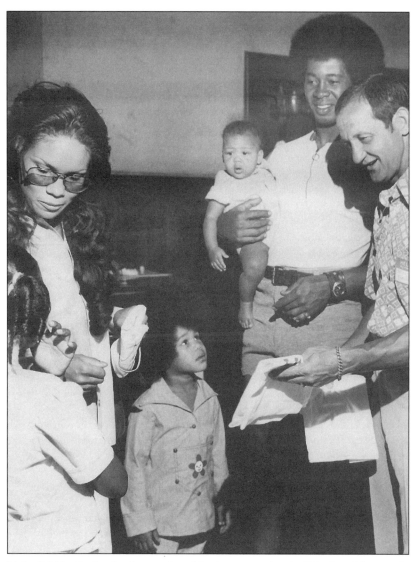

Little did Charlie Sanders know when this photo was taken in 1974 that eight-month-old daughter Mary Jo, who he was holding, would go on to become a boxing champion. Also in the photo, from left, are daughter Mia, wife Georgianna, daughter Charese, and coach Rick Forzano. *Photo courtesy of the Detroit Lions*

one anyway. It wasn't her, but the trainers, who said, "Hey, where's the sweater?" So I had to go back to the room and change sweaters.

She was the smallest girl. She weighed about 140. There were girls there who weighed 220. She broke her nose in her first fight and was in three more fights before she knew it. She asked me, "What does it mean when you rub your nose and hear things?" I said it's just gristle, don't worry about it. She was scheduled to fight on a card with Muhammad Ali's daughter two weeks after that. I'm saying that would be OK. My wife took her to get her nose X-rayed. It showed she had broken her nose and that's the last medical advice I gave her. I tried boxing once, got hit in the nose, and that's when I quit. Tears came out of my eyes and I said I'd rather play basketball.

ALL FOR ONE, ONE FOR ALL

We stood up for each other on the field and I can readily understand what happened November 2, 1936, in New York when the Lions lost to the Giants, 14-7. It was a rough game and at one point star Lions fullback Ace Gutowsky had words with Cal Hubbard, a 268-pound hulk who said he would get Ace afterwards. But Hubbard, already with a black eye from being elbowed by Lions quarterback Dutch Clark during the game, was talking with Clark as they walked off the field after the game. Gutowsky stepped up and, according to the story in the *Detroit Times* by Leo McDonnell, said: "Here I am if you want me."

Hubbard swung, but all of a sudden there was Frank Christensen, decking Hubbard with one punch. Hubbard leaped up at Gutowski, but Clark and others broke things up. "It was just my light left," Christensen, who was 30 pounds lighter than Hubbard, said.

A couple days later coach Potsy Clark sent a letter of apology to Giants coach Steve Owen. It read: "I have talked to our players about it and I assure you that the incident will not occur again. It is the first of its kind which has happened in my six years' experience in the league."

Maybe he wrote a letter of apology, but chances are he felt good about his players sticking up for each other. Hubbard, whose pro career began in 1927 with the Giants, also played for Green Bay and Pittsburgh before closing out his career back with New York in 1936. He was to go on to other fame, however, as a major league umpire—and in 1976 was inducted into the Baseball Hall of Fame while I was playing with the Lions.

NOT SO SWEET

When I joined the Lions in 1968, the quarterbacks from the previous season—veteran Milt Plum and Karl Sweetan—were gone. After hearing about some of the stories about Sweetan, I could understand why he wasn't back. Even while Joe Don Looney was making headlines with his scrapes, he was joined in 1966 by 24-year-old rookie quarterback Sweetan (1966-1967), who also seemed to be a trouble magnet. In January 1967 he was charged with assault over a fracas that took place the previous October at Sunnybrook Lanes bowling center in Sterling Heights. He was accused of punching a guy in the nose, but the man's attorney filed for dismissal of the charge and of a $10,000 damage claim.

"I was provoked into it," Sweetan said, in a *News* article January 6. The story said a woman asked Sweetan to move her belongings from another man's table and he objected. "In my estimation, he was going to hit me, so I hit him first," Sweetan said. (Two men dropped similar charges against Lions linebackers Wayne Walker and Mike Lucci from an incident November 18 in which the men claimed to have been struck by the Lions.)

20

LONG ARM OF THE LAW

LOCKER ROOM LAWYER

Charlie Bradshaw (OT, 1967-1968) was near the end of his career when I joined the Lions. He was No. 1 in the Texas bar exams and was the only player-attorney in pro football. He had his own law firm partnership in Houston. He was a locker room lawyer and became president of the NFL Players Association. He knew all the rules and regulations, what you could and couldn't do in and outside the league, so anybody who wanted legal advice would run to him. Bradshaw was very well versed and a very intelligent individual. Bradshaw began his career with the Los Angeles Rams. After three seasons he went to the Pittsburgh Steelers, before joining the Lions seven years later.

DOWNTOWN DASH

In my playing days, just about all of us from the Lions hung out at the Lindell A.C., the sports bar downtown (which has since closed). We had played an exhibition game in 1969 against the Patriots in Montreal. After flying back, we went to our training site at Cranbrook and got our cars and decided to go back downtown to the Lindell before it closed. Mel Farr and Lem Barney each owned Corvettes. I had a customized GTX convertible. They said the last one to get to the Lindell would pick up the tab.

Mel rode with Lem and Earl McCullouch rode with me. I only knew one way to get downtown and that was to come out Lahser and go down the Lodge Freeway. Mel and Lem went straight down Woodward. I remember getting on the Lodge and looking down at the speedometer and I was doing 125 m.p.h. There was a flashing light in the rear view mirror. I thought it was an ambulance and I switched lanes, but the flashers were still behind me. I pulled over to let them pass, but they pulled behind me. It was the police.

McCullouch had been in Los Angeles during the Watts riots and he readily knew it was the police and not an EMS ambulance. They made us get out of the car. Earl, having witnessed the riots in Watts, put his hands up on the roof, palms down. One policeman by me had a gun out and the other by Earl had his out, too. They asked for my driver's license, which I carried in the glove compartment. I'm not thinking and I reach for the glove box and Earl takes one hand off the roof and slaps me across the wrist. He knew the police might think I was going for a gun.

At the same time, you could hear the guns get cocked. I calmly explained my license was in the glove box. Earl was so afraid. He told the policeman to reach in there and get it. I had a North Carolina license. I explained our story. They probably should have taken us to jail, but they let us go with just a ticket for going 20 m.p.h. over the speed limit. And I had to give up my license and get a Michigan one.

TAKING STOCK

I have known some players who have sued their teams for one reason or another. It's not something new in the NFL. Former Lions standout from their early days, Clare Randolph, sued the team in May 1960 for $60,000, claiming he took 4.5 of the 250 authorized shares of the Portsmouth Spartans in lieu of back pay of $450 after the 1932 season. The team was sold to Dick Richards in 1934 for $15,000 and became the Lions.

Randolph's attorney, Sam Thorne, said in a *Times* story by George Van that the players' shares amounted to 1/50th of the franchise's value, and he asked the Michigan Securities Commission to evaluate the stock. Richards sold the franchise to Fred Mandel in 1940 for $225,000, and Mandel sold it eight years later for $250,000.

HOLLYWOOD HULLABALOO

The banner headline in the November 4, 1960, *Detroit Times* read: 'Lions Star Accused of Striking Hollywood Model.' The player involved was Carl Brettschneider. The 230-pound linebacker was accused of assault and battery by 21-year-old "Myla Miles," a five-foot-one, 125-pound woman, who said the incident took place at "The Losers," a bar on the Sunset Strip in Hollywood.

"I never saw the girl before," Brettschneider said. "I was in the place with four or five other men from the team. She scratched at me and called me names. I grabbed her wrist. She slipped and fell. We left the place."

Teammate Nick Pietrosante backed Brettschneider's version. The *Free Press* said the others there were Terry Barr, Gil Mains, and Jim Gibbons. During practice after the publicity had come out, teammates joked as Martin knocked down several passes: "That's the way, Carl, hit her again!"

The *Times* quoted an unidentified coach as saying, "This is just like old times. We had our best clubs when we were getting involved in these things…" The woman, later identified as Shirley Allen, filed suit against Brettschneider and 39 other defendants for $60,000.

CUSTODY BATTLE

He had only just finished his rookie season and a week earlier was involved in a tussle at a bar, but on January 11, 1967, quarterback Karl Sweetan became embroiled in a custody battle in Macomb County Circuit Court with his estranged wife, JoAnn, over their two children. The ex-Playboy Bunny was awarded custody if she remained a resident in the tri-county area and wouldn't get a job until the kids were in school.

The following November, Sweetan suffered a six-inch gash on his left arm after driving his fist through the storm door while trying to enter the home of his fiancé in Detroit. The police were called. Sweetan wasn't booked but got a warning. He was bandaged and at practice the next day.

21

MASCOT MINUTIAE

'KIDS' DIDN'T GROW

In the first eight years I played I thought the Lions' mascots were little kids. I never knew they were little people. I thought it was amazing that they were into their characters like they were. I never saw their faces. Eventually, I realized the "kids" weren't getting any bigger. The Lions were the only team in the league with a caricature mascot in 1934 and what was a gimmick then has remained a familiar part of the franchise.

Inside the large Lion costume, I would later find out, was Bill Baker, son of the original mascot, William "Moon" Baker. And inside the cub costume was Blanche Verghougstraete, who was nine when she started playing the role.

When the movie *Paper Lion* made its premier in October 1968 (my rookie year) at the Adams Theater downtown, among the celebrities outside were the mascots Bill Baker and Verghougstraete, the four-foot-five typesetter who by then had been playing the role for 32 years.

'MOON' MAN

The Lions' costumed mascot went over big right from the beginning, according to John Walter's story in *The Detroit News*. But the costume, worn by William "Moon" Baker, "was such a job to make" that plans to have four lions were scrapped, Walter's story said, quoting public relations man Tommy Emmet. The costume cost $300. Eventually, there would be a big lion and a "cub," which we still have today.

"It took two weeks to make the lion and Moon had to go three times to have it fitted so the head would balance on his shoulders in true lion style," Emmet said. It took 20 minutes to put the costume on, with the help of cheerleader Judy Tosha. Baker was too short to see through the lion's eyes and so he had to look out the

These three were honored in 1976 for their service to the Lions. From left, Eddie Howland, leader of the side-line "chain-gang" starting in 1940; Blanche Verhougstraete, cub mascot since 1938 (alongside full-sized mascot 'Moon' Baker and later his son, Bill); and Roy "Friday" Macklem, whose long tenure as equipment manager began in 1936. *Photo courtesy of the Detroit Lions*

mouth. Both he and Tosha worked at Great Lakes Steel, the company of one of the Lions owners. Two other cheerleaders were William Bone and Gerald Polsin.

The idea for the lion costume came from principal team owner Dick Richards, who got the idea after seeing Pittsburgh University cheerleaders dressed as panthers.

Baker, who was short, played basketball and baseball at Redford High School. He got the nickname "Moon," because at the time there was a Moon Baker who was a star athlete at Northwestern and he stood just five foot five.

TRAGIC END

Baker, who served as the Lions' lion for 27 years until his son, Bill, replaced him in 1960, was found dead on a sidewalk on Winder Street near Woodward on August 11, 1960, apparently a victim of a heart attack at age 50. He lived in Dearborn and was a parts manager for a car agency there.

Homicide detectives said Baker had a cut over his left eye and across the bridge of his nose and his glasses laying alongside him were smashed and his pockets were turned inside out. Identification was made through an appliance store receipt on him. His wallet was found under the floor mat of his car nearby, with $338 in it.

NO MORE PETS

A man in Fort Worth, Texas, wrote to GM Nick Kerbawy to offer him his 20-day-old lion cub as a mascot. Kerbawy was enthralled with the idea and talked to his wife, Antha, about it. "Now, Nick, I have three cats and a dog to amuse you and our six-year-old son, but I won't be a babysitter to a lion cub," she was quoted as saying in a March 3, 1952, newspaper article. Kerbawy phoned Frank McInnis, director of the Detroit Zoo, who told him he'd have to bottle feed the cub milk four times a day. Kerbawy called his secretary and said, "I am not in the market for a lion cub as a mascot. I just hate to feed baby lions."

MILESTONE MOMENTS

It would take a whole separate book to recount Lions milestones, good or bad, and each season more are reached. Today's young fans, and even players, may not be cognizant of who's who and what was what in the early days of the franchise, but as a Lions player and later radio game analyst, I felt it was important to know at least some of the more pertinent history from that first season.

First Game

The first Lions game was at home, Sunday, September 23, 1934, against the New York Giants at University of Detroit Stadium. The Lions won 9-0 before 12,000 spectators. After a scoreless first half, quarterback Dutch Clark scored first for Detroit on a 20-yard drop kick for three points in the third quarter. The score stayed that way until just before the game ended when Roy "Father" Lumpkin raced 45 yards for a touchdown with an interception return.

(Lumpkin, from Georgia Tech, played in the 1929 Rose Bowl game made famous by the 70-yard wrong-way run of Roy Riegals of Southern Cal, who was tackled on his own 1-yard line by one of his own players.)

Tickets for the inaugural game cost between 40 cents and $2. Programs were 10 cents. Among the advertisements in the newspapers of the day was one for a sale at Finsterwald's for suits and overcoats for $14.95. And there was one for Old Murphy Whiskey for $1.75 a quart, "Detroit's popular bourbon before Prohibition."

Nickname Origin

Cy Huston, vice president and general manager of the Lions in 1934, explained to the news media why the former "Spartans" of Portsmouth, Ohio, were named "Lions" on moving to Detroit: "The lion is the monarch of the jungle and we hope to be the monarch of the league," he said. "It is our ambition to make the lion as famous as the Detroit ball club has made the tiger."

23

MILITARY COMMITMENTS

LAST MEASURE OF DEVOTION

I used to grouse about what a pain I thought it was to have to serve in the Army Reserves while I was playing football for the Lions. But who has a right to complain after finding out that six of my predecessors were killed during World War II? That was 26 percent of the 23 NFL players who were killed in the war. Those Lions (or Portsmouth Spartans or Detroit Panthers) who gave up their lives in the line of duty were:

- *Lt. Charlie Behan, an end for Detroit from DeKalb in 1942, was killed on Okinawa, May 18, 1945.*
- *Lt. Chuck Braidwood, an end for Portsmouth in 1930, was a member of the Red Cross and was killed in the South Pacific in the winter of 1944-1945.*
- *Sgt. Alex Ketzko, a Lions tackle in 1943 and a former Michigan State player, was killed in France on December 23, 1944.*
- *Capt. Lee Kizzire, a Lions fullback and linebacker in 1937, was killed when his plane was shot down near New Guinea in 1943.*
- *Chief Specialist Gus Sonnenberg, a back with the 1926 Panthers team in Detroit, died of illness in 1944 at Bethesda Naval Hospital in Maryland.*
- *Lt. Chet Wetterlund, a halfback with Detroit in 1942, was killed in a plane crash off the coast of New Jersey September 5, 1944.*

SUPER HERO BRITT

Maybe Lions should take a team history class when they come out of college or over from another team. If I had taken one then I would have known that there was a Lions player who won the Medal of Honor and another who won the Navy Cross.

Players strive today for a Super Bowl ring, and there's no military draft to worry about.

While the Lions struggled mightily, and not very successfully, to field a decent team during the World War II years, their roster was decimated. They had 59 players in military service from 1941 to 1945. In terms of full seasons missed by active players, the Lions had six gone in 1941; 23 in 1942; 45 in 1943; 54 in 1944; and 42 in 1945. And that doesn't count staff members, such as general manager Graham P. Smith, who was a Marine.

One who didn't make it back in the same condition as he was as a player in 1941 as a six-foot-four, 220-pound rookie two-way end from the University of Arkansas was Maurice Britt. He probably wasn't far off from matching Audie Murphy in decorations.

Britt was awarded the Medal of Honor and had an arm amputated due to his wounds. He was awarded the Purple Heart (with cluster due to being wounded more than once) and also the Army's second highest award, the Distinguished Service Cross, as well as a Silver Star and the British Military Cross.

The hero from the 3rd Infantry Division earned the nation's highest award for valor November 10, 1943, in Italy, receiving multiple wounds in the process. His citation "for conspicuous gallantry and intrepidity at the risk of his life above and beyond the call of duty" read, in part:

"Disdaining enemy hand grenades and close range machine pistol, machine gun and rifle [fire], Lt. Britt inspired and led a handful of his men in repelling a bitter counterattack by approximately 100 Germans against his company positions.... During the intense firefight, Lt. Britt's canteen and field glasses were shattered; a bullet pierced his side; his chest, face, and hands were covered with grenade wounds.

"Despite his wounds, for which he refused to accept medical attention until ordered to do so... he personally killed five and wounded an unknown number of Germans, wiped out one enemy machine gun crew, fired five clips of carbine and an undetermined amount of M1 rifle ammunition, and threw 32 fragmentation grenades...."

Britt was an honor student at Arkansas, and before his brief stint with the Lions he was sports editor of the *Arkansas Traveler*.

TOUGHER THAN FOOTBALL

Imagine how tough a player John Tripson of Mission, Texas, might have been for Detroit had he not gone off to fight in the Navy during World War II. Edgar Hayes, writing in the February 24, 1943, edition of the *Detroit Times*, pieced the following information together from November 7, 1942, when Tripson was with a scout and raider party in the invasion of North Africa. His actions that day probably saved the lives of hundreds of American troops, and the 6-3, 220-pound former tackle from Mississippi State was awarded the Navy Cross.

"Deprived of weapons when his landing boat blew up, John Robert Tripson, rough, tough tackle who played with the Detroit Lions in 1941, today was credited with having strangled two Vichy French sentries with his bare hands."

Tripson was in the first Higgins boat leaving a transport and the landing craft of 20 sailors was hit by artillery fired from an old Moorish fort. Only eight men landed alive and all lost their equipment. The men were supposed to light flares to aid the invasion. The men seized machine guns and turned them on the Vichy French defenders who were charging down the beach. One of the boats behind Tripson's included Phil Buckley of the Cleveland Rams. He was feared lost, but survived.

OTHER HEROES, TOO

We had a former Marine on our team, wide receiver Phil Odle, but I didn't realize that our special team's coach, Jim Martin, not only was a former Marine, but a decorated one, as well. Martin, the guard from Notre Dame and great Lions linebacker and kicker from 1951-1961, won a Bronze Star at Tinian in the South Pacific for swimming ashore to get information on the upcoming Marines landing 15 days later. We didn't talk that much, but I suppose his tattoo might have given me a clue. He was a low-key guy, but you didn't want to mess with him.

Ensign John Tripson of the Navy (and ex-Lions tackle), second from right, was among those here in 1943 receiving the Navy Cross for gallantry in the invasion of North Africa. To his right is another ex-NFL player, Ensign Robert Halperin, who played for the Brooklyn Dodgers. *Photo courtesy of the Detroit Lions*

Another decorated Lion was superstar running back Byron "Whizzer" White, later a member of the U.S. Supreme Court. He earned a Bronze Star while a lieutenant in the Navy. Among the other well-known Lions who served was quarterback and Heisman Trophy winner Frank Sinkwich.

The post-war Lions rosters were packed with WWII vets, many of whom weren't active players before the war started. Some of them I saw from year to year when we'd have a homecoming game for former players.

Aldo Forte, an ex-Chicago Bears guard, was a Navy lieutenant who earned four Bronze Stars and who managed a jewelry store in Detroit before joining the Lions briefly in 1946. They sent him back to Chicago the same season and he closed out his career in 1947 with the Green Bay Packers.

John Treadway, a tackle from Hardin-Simmons who played on the 1949 Lions, was another bonafide war hero. He was a Navy lieutenant commander who earned the Silver Star, Purple Heart, and eight battle stars.

John Mattiford, a guard on the 1941 Lions, served as assistant coach for the First Allied Airborne team. Another paratrooper was Frank Gigonis, a fullback and linebacker on the 1942 squad. He was player-coach for the 508th Parachute Regiment. Earl "Jug" Girard of two Lions title teams in the 1950s, also was a paratrooper.

The Lions' 1947 training camp roster featured 44 players who had been in military service: 13 Navy, 12 Army Air Force, 11 Army, seven Marines, and one Coast Guard. Four of them earned Purple Hearts for their wounds.

Gus Cifelli, a tackle from Notre Dame who played with the Lions from 1951-1953 and later became a prominent judge in the area, served in the Marines for 31 months. The machine gunner was discharged because of his wounds. He later became a boxing instructor.

Vince Banonis, UD star from 1939-1941, played for the Chicago Cardinals in 1942 before the war interrupted his career. After 41 months in the service, the Navy lieutenant returned to play for the Cardinals from 1946-1950, then with the Lions from 1951-1953. He was the center on the Lions' 1952 and 1953 World Championship teams and in 1975 was elected to the Michigan Sports Hall of Fame.

DRAFT BOARD WORRIES

The Vietnam war was going on when I was drafted—by the Lions, that is. As a college student at Minnesota, I was exempt if I kept my grades up. I dropped below a 1.0 grade-point average and my old man said I wouldn't be coming home, I'd be going to Vietnam. But within one quarter I had my average up to a B+.

After graduation I had to be reclassified and probably would have been drafted, but I soon got married and we had a child, and that moved me lower on the list. I joined the Army Reserves, and so did Jim Yarbrough and Garo Yepremian. The three of us were in the 323rd Medical Hospital Division and we'd have to go to meetings on Beech-Daly Road in Redford. Lem Barney was in the Navy Reserves.

My basic training was at Fort Polk, Louisana. I wouldn't want to wish it on anyone. There were snakes. It was hot. It was the worst experience I had in my life. The second worst was going to Fort Sam Houston in Texas for six weeks. I came back to the Lions at about 205-207 pounds. My breakfast down there was a Coca Cola and a packet of peanut butter Nabs. I couldn't eat the food they served. It was just horrible. Horrible.

Every now and then you'd get a package from home and hope when it got there it wasn't rotten. Other than that you'd end up eating green eggs and bacon floating in grease. So you'd go down to the vending machine and buy pop and a pack of Nabs.

The hardest part for me was maintaining my Afro, because in Reserve units you had to wear your hair short. But the style then was the Afro. Every time we had a weekend meeting I'd wash my hair with Tide and, for some reason, it would shrink down to nothing. I had to find a way to tuck it in my hat so I was presentable enough.

Every month or every other month we had a weekend in the Reserves. They'd schedule it when it wasn't football season. They gave you some flexibility there. We probably got away with a lot more than we should have.

EARLIER DRAFT CONCERNS

Some 14 months before the bombing of Pearl Harbor by the Japanese on December 7, 1941, put the U.S. into World War II, local draft boards were gearing up for war because it was raging in Europe and elsewhere. Included among the signups were Lions players. One newspaper photo, under the headline, 'Detroit's Athletes Flock to Registration Booths as Uncle Sam's Draft Boards Swing Into Action,' showed Grosse Pointe Shores' registrar Norbert Denk getting the names of five Lions on the dotted line: John Morlock, Bill Radovich, Tony Calvelli, Harry Smith, and Paul Moore.

Joe Manzo, a tackle from Boston College, planned to play with Detroit in 1941 and was due to play in two all-star games, but his draft board announced in July he would be inducted August 2. He did return and played one year in the league, for the Lions in 1945.

In August 1943, the *Free Press* ran a photo of former Lions coach Bill Edwards, who was a lieutenant, and four other Navy officers—all coaches—at the Navy Pre-Flight School near San Francisco. The school's football team had quite an experienced coaching staff.

NO 1-A'S WANTED

Perhaps sick and tired of losing good players to the armed forces at the start of World War II, Lions owner Fred Mandel issued an edict in January 1942 stating: "Pro football will roll along this fall despite the war, but the Detroit Lions won't sign one player who is suited for Army duty." He already had said goodbye to nine Lions from his 1941 roster, the latest being standout tackle Emil Uremovich.

"Next fall's Lions will be men who are not considered available for Army duty because of dependents or physical disabilities," Mandel said, in Lew Walter's story in the *Detroit Times*. "They'll be doing their share in defense work, in maintaining their families, and in providing amusement for what otherwise might be a drab existence for many." The government had asked the NFL to carry on with its season to help boost morale and Mandel said, "We're going to do our best."

A month later, the former team trainer, Abe Kushner, enlisted in the Navy and became a Hospital Apprentice First Class. When he walked into the recruiting office, on duty was ex-Lion back Paul Moore, a coxswain assigned to Federal Building Forces.

In April 1943, Mandel reversed his approach to player acquisition, apparently figuring it would be better to draft top-notch players and hope to get them after their military service than sub-par ones just to fill the roster. So in the draft they took Sinkwich as their top pick, despite the fact he was in the Marines. Each team selected 30 players that season because of the war, rather than 20 as before. Teams had to almost guess who might be drafted.

Mandel's gamble on the former Heisman-winning quarterback paid off, and five months later he was in training camp, having been discharged September 11 for what an Augusta, Georgia, newspaper said was flat feet, a heart murmur, and high blood pressure.

LATER DRAFTS GRAB STARS

Wally Triplett's draft board in New Kensington, Pennsylvania, ordered him to report to the Army in November 1950, depriving the Lions of another good player. During the 1950 season he had set an NFL record by returning four kickoffs for 294 yards in the Lions' 65-24 loss to the Rams. He had a 97-yard return for Detroit's first touchdown, and set up a 47-yard Doak Walker field goal with a 74-yard return. His others were for 81 and 42 yards.

In February 1954, running back Gene Gedman got drafted and was shown in a *Times* photo having his ears examined by a doctor at Fort Wayne. A few weeks later during the early days of his two-year service time, he showed up in another *Times* photo wearing a helmet and holding a rifle.

Terry Barr left in November 1961 for two weeks of military duty at Fort Knox, Kentucky, with the National Guard, but expected to get passes to play in two upcoming games. The Army also summoned guard John Gordy for duty to Fort Lewis, Washington. He missed one game, but played the final two.

Frank Sinkwich, who received his Heisman Trophy in 1942 while in the Marines, was drafted the following season by Detroit despite his service obligations.
Photo courtesy of the Detroit Lions

RIOT DUTY

During the era when civil rights demonstrations were trying to change the face of America, Detroit was one of the cities hit with a devastating riot. Lions John Henderson and Tom Myers, both called to National Guard duty, found themselves patrolling Detroit streets in July 1967.

"We're doing what must be done," said Henderson, an end who starred at Michigan. "I just hope and pray that none of us will ever have to use a gun on our own Americans."

Henderson had just returned from four and a half months with the Guard in Fort Lewis, Washington, and had gone to only two workouts in Lions training camp before being ordered to report to the Light Guard Armory for active duty. Both he and quarterback Myers went on patrols along Grand River Avenue and around 12th Street.

24

MUSICAL INCLINATIONS

FIGHT SONG COMPOSER

I'm not a fan of the Lions' fight song, "Gridiron Heroes." I never understood it and never learned it. But, heck, I didn't even know our fight song in college. I wish the Lions would come up with a more upbeat, modern song, but that one has been around a long time.

Dr. Graham T. Overgard, who composed it, was the subject in the fall of 1954 of a feature in *Guest* magazine, distributed to hotels in the area. It called him a "unique talent and organizing genius" for getting more than 500 musicians and other participants involved in each half-time show at the Lions games. At least five bands would be involved, and sometimes seven or eight, plus a hundred majorettes. The show would be new each week, and over the course of a six-game home season more than 3,000 different persons would participate.

REED 'PLAYS FOR JESUS'

I've seen Joey Harrington (QB, 2002-) play the piano and Corey Harris (S, 2002-2003) play the guitar, but there weren't many in my era who were interested in singing or playing an instrument. One who was, though, was quarterback Joe Reed (1974-1979), whose good singing voice prompted him to make several recordings. Among them were two gospel albums, *The Lion in Me*, and *Have You Kissed Any Frogs Today?* The cover of that record said, in part, "When Joe Reed picks up his guitar and begins to sing, it's hard to believe that the same man who is singing so beautifully could possibly spend his weekends amidst the violence of an NFL football game.... The decal on his helmet is of the Detroit Lions—but in truth, Joe Reed plays for Jesus."

I still have that album somewhere down my basement.

JAZZ MAN

Harris owned a Nashville-based record label, SYBE Records (Strong Young Black Entrepreneur), and in 1998 released a CD entitled *Unrestricted* under the stage name of C.LOH. He also was owner of a jazz and R&B club in Nashville called "Somethin' Live."

QB HOSTS CONCERT

Harrington hosted a summer concert in Portland, Oregon, in 2003 as the signature fund-raiser for the Harrington Family Foundation. The concert featured the Blues Travelers and Jason Mraz. Third Eye Blind and the Pat McGee Band headlined the concert the next year. The foundation was established to promote the education, safety, and welfare of children. In 2003, Harrington, who started playing the piano early in his childhood, displayed his musical talents in ABC TV's *Monday Night Football at the Mic*, an on-line fan voting contest involving NFL players with music abilities.

SAX AND SAMBAS?

Ken Jenkins (RB, 1983-1984) studied acting while at Bucknell and played the saxophone. Also, with his sister, Roxanne, he owned a dance studio in Washington, D.C.

RUNS IN THE FAMILY

Karl Bernard (RB, 1987-1988) was an accomplished singer. He performed the national anthem prior to a Detroit Pistons basketball game. Bernard had an aunt who was a soprano for the Berlin Opera in Germany.

LIGHTS OUT

Eight-year Lions receiver Johnnie Morton (1994-2001) appeared in a music video, "Turn Out the Lights," with Motown R&B artist Shanice Wilson in 1994. During the off-season he was involved in acting, screen writing, and television production.

OX A LOMBARDO FAN

Just as some of today's players might tire of listening to hip-hop music in the locker rooms, back in 1934, Ox Emerson (OL-LB, 1934-1937) also wasn't attuned to modern popular music on the upbeat side. He preferred the melodic sounds of easy-going dance bands of Wayne King and Guy Lombardo.

"They're above the hi-de-ho stuff" (of Cab Calloway) he said, in a *Detroit Times* article by Leo Macdonell. "When you're waltzing with King, you're waltzing."

Macdonell said Emerson "gets somewhat annoyed with some of the Cab Calloway stuff preferred by more uncouth Lions." Also, the reporter said, Emerson didn't like movies "because they're trashy."

HILLSDALE'S OWN

Bob Rowe (FB, 1934), a member of the first Lions team, used to entertain teammates by playing lively tunes on the piano after team dinners. At Colgate University he was involved in drama and had an ambition to be a playwright.

Colgate was the champion of the East in 1932, going 9-0, and alumni were dismayed that Pittsburgh, instead, got the bid to play in the Rose Bowl game. A famous line then by Colgate alums was that their team was "unbeaten, untied, and uninvited," a line others would borrow in future years.

Rowe was on the staff of Amos Alonzo Stagg at the University of the Pacific when Cy Huston asked him to play for the Lions (football, not piano) and he jumped at the chance. The Hillsdale native was the only Michigan-born member of that 1934 squad.

COUNTRY GUYS

Equipment manager Roy "Friday" Macklem was pictured in the June 7, 1959 *News* wearing country and western garb and carrying a guitar as he boarded a bus that was called a rolling showboat for a tour around the state sponsored by a Detroit brewery. Macklem was the Lions equipment man since the Dutch Clark era. In the off-season he worked in a factory. "The players always said I ought to be in pictures," he said. "This is the nearest thing to it."

Also in the 1950s, tackle Thurman McGraw (1950-1954) was a favorite entertainer at Lions functions as a country and western singer.

25

NICKNAMES

Some of my favorite nicknames of Lions were: Lem "Stroll" Barney, Mel "Pine" Farr, Coach "Wayno" Fontes, Tommy "Chink" Vaughn, Earl "Sweets" McCullouch, Greg "Gomer" Landry, and Bill "Chisel" Munson.

There were some other clever nicknames over the years. Some were natural derivations from their given names, but others came from who knows where. There was a "Bullet Bob" Westfall and a "Bullet Bill" Bowman; a Howard "Hopalong" Cassady, a Dave "Hoppy" Middleton, and a Harry "Hippity" Hop. There was an Ed "Fluff" Flanagan and a William "Freeze" Frizzell.

There were a couple "Bubbas" (Al Baker, William Paris) and a "Buddha" Bill Cottrell; a "Whiskey" (Joe Robb) and a "Jack Daniels" (Errol Mann). There was a Cotton called "King" (Craig Cotton) and a Price (Charles) nicknamed "Cotton."

There are just too many nicknames to mention, but here are a few more, ones that might not seem to belong to tough football players: "Queenie" (Dutch Clark), "Twinks" (Gene Cronin), "Lamb Eyes" (Red Stacey), and "Sugar Bear" (Homer Elias).

26

ORNERY OPPONENTS

BRUISER BUTKUS

Although linebacker Dick Butkus of the Chicago Bears went to Illinois and I went to Minnesota, both Big Ten schools, I never played against him in college. But I'd heard about him. There were pictures in magazines showing Butkus running through forests and tackling trees. So my rookie year I started to wonder what the hell I was getting myself into.

We were getting ready to play this animal and coach Joe Schmidt was walking around and giving a speech and patting everyone. I was so nervous. Both legs were moving and I was trying to keep from hyperventilating. Joe walked over to me and was getting ready to pat me. He looked at me and I was just staring into space. He backed away and said he didn't think he needed to talk to me.

It was already established that Butkus would pick someone out who was pretty good. If it wasn't me, it was running back Mel Farr. One he loved to take out was center Ed Flanagan, because he lined up over him. He used to just physically beat Ed up. But Ed never complained, and I think that really ticked Butkus off.

I remember one time he wiped out Flanagan, quarterback Bill Munson, running back Altie Taylor, and Farr in the same game. There was a time he chased Taylor up into the stands because he ran out of bounds and wouldn't let him hit him. Altie came back into the huddle and said, "Hey, this man is crazy."

The officials were afraid of Butkus and afraid to say anything to him. My rookie year when we played him in Detroit, well, you get fired up for someone like that. I remember saying if this guy tries to tackle me, I'm not going to go down. I caught a pass and was struggling with it and Butkus got me in a headlock. I was still struggling and he took his two fingers and was gouging at my eyes. I said to myself, "Hell, you're married. You've got a kid. You better go down." To this day when I see him I say, "You were a dirty player."

We'd be in a huddle and hear screaming and yelling and it would be Butkus. He might have a chunk of meat in his mouth and it would be a piece of your leg or something. I'd refer to him as a maladjusted kid. When you talk to him now he'd say, "Nah, I wasn't like that." You'd play with him at the Pro Bowl and he'd be great. He just hated anybody who wasn't on his team. He was an animal who actually hated the opponent. He was going to do anything he could to intimidate somebody, to hurt somebody. It finally caught up to him. People said let's get to him first before he gets to us.

SNAP DECISION

In another Butkus-related tale, we had a guy named David Thompson who we drafted and who supposedly had the fastest velocity on his snaps. I had found out in practice that I had a knack for long snaps and on Saturday mornings I'd compete with him and sometimes I'd even beat him. Well, little did I know I was setting myself up for a situation that I wasn't going to appreciate. Thompson was traded, and our center, Flanagan, took over the long-snapping responsibilities and I became the backup.

Well, we were playing a game in Chicago and Flanagan got injured at a critical point and it looked like I'd have to come in and snap for a crucial field goal try late in the game when we were down by two points. I went over to Flanagan and basically pleaded with him, saying, "Look, do you want us to win this game? If so, you'd better go in there and snap that ball, because there's no way I'm going to let Butkus get a running shot at me and take my head off."

I had my share of battles with Butkus over the course of my first three or four years in the league. Well, Flanagan went in, snapped the ball, and Errol Mann ended up kicking a field goal and we won. That was about as nervous as I've ever been. It wasn't a matter of Butkus blocking a field goal. He wanted to knock my head off and I knew it. So Flanagan pulled me out of a tough position.

MCCOY GETS HIS DUE

The Green Bay Packers drafted Notre Dame defensive tackle Mike McCoy as their first pick in 1970, and when we played them there that year it was bitterly cold. He had a unique physique, with small shoulders and a behind twice the size of a normal person. After an interception, McCoy tried to blind-side me with a block. I had my back turned and didn't see him, but I could hear him. He was like a rhino coming at me. He went over the top of my shoulder and then started laughing at me.

I remember going to Fred Carr, the linebacker for Green Bay out of Arizona, and making the comment to him that McCoy shouldn't have laughed at me. Later I went to our quarterback and asked him to throw a screen pass, one that required me to block McCoy. We were going to lose the game anyway, and I had the philosophy that if you weren't going to win, at least you should take a scalp. I had about a 15-yard running start at McCoy and was going to crack-back block him low. But I got a look at that wide behind and changed my mind and decided to go for his facemask. When he got up he was spitting broken teeth. The next time I saw Mike McCoy he was doing a dental commercial.

REVENGE AGAINST EX-LION

The most hated player on the Minnesota Vikings when we were having our frustrating years against them in the 1970s was linebacker Wally Hilgenberg. He was a Lion in 1964-1966 and resented that the Lions cut him. When I came in my rookie year he wanted to take his animosity out on me. For about the first four years it was cheap shot after cheap shot after cheap shot. He came all the way from the other side of the field in one game to cheap shot me and I think he got suspended.

I remember playing the Vikings at Tiger Stadium and I went up to the referee and told him to watch that guy because he was gouging at my eyes on the snap of the ball. I warned the ref that if it happened on the first play I was pretty much going to swing at him. So on the first play he gouged my eyes and somehow my fist hit right between the opening of his face mask. I didn't realize the end result and later in the game I was down in my stance and, drip, drip, drip. I realized it was blood, coming from his nose. I had broken his nose.

It was a problem because we played the next game in Minnesota. The Vikings actually kept him out of the game. I don't know whether the commissioner got involved or they just held him out, but there was no confrontation. It was like there was a bounty going back and forth and we had a bounty on him.

I was in chapel service prior to that game and I was ripping out chairs. Guys up there were talking about God and I'm thinking about killing Wally Hilgenberg on the field. It got to the point where it was so overwhelming I had to get up and walk out. Guys used to hate to sit in chapel services next to me. My rookie year I'd get nervous and wouldn't eat from Saturday noon until Monday. I came in at 250 pounds as a rookie tight end and ended up at 205 because I had this nervousness and couldn't hold food down.

In chapel every Sunday before the game I'd go in and hyperventilate and bounce up and down. I think I made other people around me nervous. You'd look around and guys would be sitting in the corners and I'd be by myself. I'd listen to the chaplain and I'd still have that nervousness and that hyperventilation. I had that even years later when I'd watch my daughter get ready for her boxing matches.

Hilgenberg and I eventually made up as "friends," although we had no verbal commitment that we would cut things out. We had our matches, that's for sure.

27

OUTSIDE THE LINES

It may be difficult for some fans to imagine their favorite players doing something other than playing football. But athletes can be as well-rounded or complex as anyone else when they're not between the white lines. Lions over the years have been involved in many special activities, charitable, athletic, or otherwise, including military service or even full-blown occupations, before they started their pro careers. Some of my contemporaries had some interesting activities:

SNOW AND ICE GUYS

Could anyone imagine me playing hockey? Well, when I was a freshman at Minnesota I enrolled in an ice skating class taught by Johnny Mariucci. He was the Gophers' hockey coach and used to be a star with the Chicago Black Hawks. (He also happens to be Lions coach Steve Mariucci's uncle.) Apparently I impressed him enough with my skating that he asked me to try out for the hockey team, but I declined.

One of our wide receivers, the five-foot-eight Jeff Campbell (1990-1993) from Colorado was ranked one of the top 25 prep hockey players in the country when he was a student at Battle Mountain High in Vail, Colorado. In track there he was two-time state champion in the 100- and 200-meter dashes. He ran the 40-yard dash in 4.37 seconds. Eric Sanders, an offensive lineman (1986-1992), meanwhile, was on the ski team at Wooster High in Reno, Nevada, He didn't play football until his junior year at Nevada-Reno.

BASEBALL GUYS

Besides Bruce Maher and Bobby Layne, other Lions dabbled in pro baseball. D.J. Dozier (RB, 1991), who in football was the first player in Penn State history to lead the team in rushing four consecutive years, also played baseball in the New York

Mets minor league system for four seasons and some time with the major league club in 1992. Jimmy Giles (TE, 1986), who spent most of his football career with Tampa Bay, played professional baseball in the summer of 1976 after being chosen in the 12th round of the baseball draft by the Los Angeles Dodgers. He was primarily a third baseman with Bellingham (Washington) of the Class A Northwest League. In Tampa he owned People's Optical, an eye care center.

DIMPLED BALL GUYS

Gus Frerotte (QB, 1999) had a hole in one in 1997 while golfing in Coeur D'Alene, Idaho. A year earlier, Jason Hanson (PK, 1992-) won the "Longest Drive" contest in the Lions' golf outing, ripping the ball 290 yards down the middle of the fairway. Dick LeBeau (CB, 1959-1972) won the NFL Players golf tournament in 1967, and Ray Oldham (DB, 1980-1982), a 1-handicap golfer, won that tournament twice. Bill Schroeder (WR, 2002-2003) was a part-time wildlife art dealer and also an active golfer. He won a local qualifier of the 2001 RE/MAX World Long Drive Championship in Madison, Wisconsin, with a drive of 357 yards.

ENTERTAINMENT OPTIONS

Robert Bailey (CB, 1997-1999, 2001) appeared on the soap opera, *The Young and the Restless*. Russ Bolinger (G, 1976-1982) appeared in a couple football-oriented movies, including *North Dallas Forty*. Lomas Brown (OT, 1985-1995) during one off-season appeared in the nationally syndicated TV show *Win, Lose or Draw*. While with the Lions, Brown was a partner in a computer service company, and owned an auto and equipment leasing franchise.

Rusty Hilger (QB, 1988), in the off-season before 1989 training camp, served as color commentator for the Pro Football Arm Wrestling Championships later televised on ESPN. He also worked with various charity organizations through his own personal promotional company and he participated in the Pomona Winter Nationals drag racing event. After his playing days, Wayne Walker (LB, 1958-1972) went on to become a successful sportscaster, getting his start in Detroit and then heading to the West Coast.

Rodney Peete (QB, 1989-1993), who got a degree in communications, worked as a baseball color analyst on a California cable station. He also worked with an organization called Athletes and Entertainers for Kids.

Roy Williams (WR, 2004-), the Lions' top draft choice in 2004, played a role in a movie, *Friday Night Lights*, starring Billy Bob Thornton, based on a book that portrays a football season at his high school, Odessa Permian in Texas. His older brother, Lloyd Hill, was on the team depicted in the book. Roy Williams's role is as an assistant coach at the school's rival, Midland Lee. He has one line—"He ain't going to play, Coach."

John Small (DT, 1973-1974) operated a Christian entertainment center in Augusta, Georgia, called "The First Step." And Leonard Thompson (WR, 1975-1986 was owner and chairman of the board of radio station KSUN in Phoenix, Arizona. He also was co-chairman of a celebrity golf tournament in 1985 in Phoenix that raised some $20,000 for the Make-A-Wish Foundation.

OTHER SPECIALTIES

Other players over the decades have had interesting non-football inclinations or occupations. Right from the start, the Lions as an organization emphasized making its players part of the community by finding them off-season jobs in the area. That hadn't changed two decades later and *Newsweek* magazine wrote an article about it, quoting PR director Nick Kerbawy: "We want them to continue a close, active interest in the club after their playing days." The article spoke of the Lions Alumni Club, organized in 1950 and with membership of 600. Kerbawy called them "600 extra scouts and 600 extra publicity agents."

As for my contemporaries, their outside-the-lines activities besides those I've already mentioned ran the gamut from staid and white collar, to gritty blue collar. Here are some of them:

Tight end Stephen Alexander (2004-) has been an avid motorcycle rider since he was a teenager, enjoying both off-road trail riding and cruising down the nation's highways. He had a chance to ride his motorcycle with a pro Supercross competitor and also an X-Games gold medallist for a segment on FOX TV's *NFL Under the Helmet*.

Defensive end John Baker (1968) was involved in rehabilitation program with inmates of a correctional institution in North Carolina and spearheaded a drive to provide religious facilities for prisoners.

Before going to Wayne State University, Tom Beer (LB, 1994-1996) spent two years working in his stepfather's commercial fishing fleet.

Punter Mike Black (1983-1987) owned and operated Phoenix Asphalt Paving Company in Arizona. One of his uncles was former Chicago Bears quarterback Virgil Carter.

Cornerback Luther Bradley (1978-1981) worked in the New York office of Merrill Lynch as a stockbroker.

Running back Dexter Bussey (1974-1984) invested in a franchise business, Mail Boxes Etc. USA, during the off-season. He was among a number of people chosen Michiganian of the Year in 1982, and fans voted him as the Lions Man of the Year in 1981.

Linebacker Paul Butcher (1986-1988), a mechanical engineering graduate from Wayne State University in Detroit, was working as a part-time doorman and bouncer at Galligan's, a downtown lounge, when the Lions called on him to try out. He was nicknamed "Dr. Psycho" at WSU and became a standout on special teams.

End Gail Cogdill (1960-1968) worked for Wayne National Life Insurance Company.

Quarterback Joe Ferguson (1985-1987) owned a single-engine Cessna that he piloted during the off-season for business and recreational trips.

Offensive tackle Rockne Freitas (1968-1977), of Kailua, Hawaii, worked in the Hawaii House of Representatives in the off-season. His hobbies included skin-diving and weight lifting.

After high school, defensive end Larry Hand (1964-1977) became a bricklayer for two years to finance his education at Appalachian State.

During the off-season, center-guard Hessley Hempstead (1995-1997) worked in the marketing department of General Motors' Cadillac World Headquarters in suburban Detroit.

Defensive back Demetrious Johnson (1983-1986), a Missouri grad with a degree in counseling psychology, owned the Supreme Clean Maintenance company, which cleaned industrial, residential, and apartment complexes. He also was part owner of Visions Consultants, which represented pro athletes in football, basketball, and soccer.

Defensive tackle James A. Jones (1999-2000) was co-owner of Jones's Tire Service in his hometown of Davenport, Iowa.

While a student at San Jose State, running back Rick Kane (1977-1983, 1985) was a locker room guard for the San Francisco 49ers during Monte Clark's year as coach there. While with the Lions, he owned a business, Lifter's Gym, in Pontiac. And another running back, Kane's teammate Horace King (RB, 1975-1983), taught in the Pontiac school system.

Fullback Cory Schlesinger (1995-) drove in demolition derbies for three years. Defensive tackle teammate Dan Wilkinson (2003-), meanwhile, didn't demolish cars, he collected them, many of which would be prime candidates for the annual Detroit-area Woodward Dream Cruise each August. Among them have been two 1970 Cadillacs, a 1966 Cadillac, and a 1965 Buick Riviera.

Center Jon Morris (1975-1977) was a partner in a food brokerage firm in Boston. His father was Washington bureau correspondent for the *New York Times*. Former All-Big Ten running back Tom Nowatzke (1965-69) of Indiana, Detroit's No. 1 draft pick in 1965, raised show horses as a hobby.

Quarterback Frank Reich (1997-1998) owned a boot shop with his former Maryland roommate, Boomer Esiason. He also owned Pro Display, a company based in Charlotte, North Carolina, that made wooden toys and memorabilia cases. And another ex-QB, Sam Wyche (1974), owned a sporting goods store in Greenville, South Carolina.

My old coach, Joe Schmidt (LB, 1953-1965); (head coach, 1967-1972), in 1957 became the Lions players' representative in the newly formed NFL Players Association. He also formed a bachelor's club on the Lions in 1953, along with Carl Karilivacz and Harley Sewell. Schmidt's brother, John, played for the Pittsburgh Steelers in 1940.

GYNECOLOGIST TEAM PHYSICIAN?

Although his career was a decade before mine, I heard about Dave Middleton (E, 1955-1960) and can't imagine how tough it must have been to go to medical school while playing for the Lions. He was a graduate of Auburn who went to Tennessee for medical school and became a doctor. During the 1960 season, his sixth and last, he got a leave of absence from his internship at the University of Michigan. He would need to spend four years of internship and then four years of residency. That made him quite the interesting story, not just locally but when the team visited other cities.

In October 1960 Philadelphia *Daily News* writer Jack McKinney wrote a feature on Middleton and apparently asked whether there was any chance of him becoming the Lions' team physician. Replied Middleton: "Hardly, I'm taking residency in obstetrics and gynecology."

Middleton said football was a welcome change of pace from the books in medical school, "but even more important were the financial benefits. Without my football income, my wife probably would have had to go to work and still we'd have been up to our ears in debt." He was able to play for the Lions while at Tennessee because the university switched to a quarter semester system.

He wasn't the only Lion, though, who became a doctor. Ben Paolucci (T, 1959) was a local product from Wayne State University in Detroit where he won four letters in football and captained the team his final two years, Paolucci completed medical school at Chicago College of Osteopathic Medicine in 1964. He became a general surgeon in 1968 and has been the team doctor of basketball's Detroit Pistons since 1972.

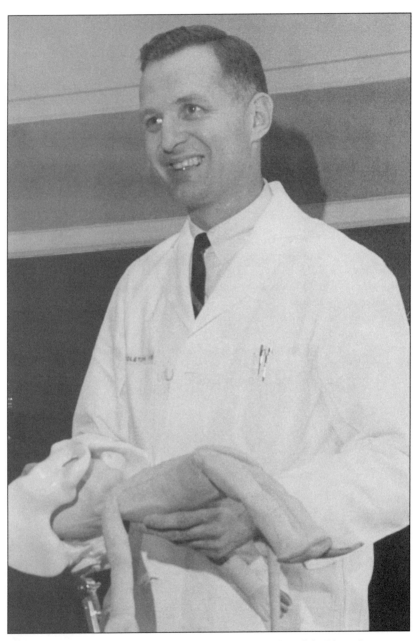

End Dave Middleton was in medical school while a member of the Lions. Someone asked him why he didn't become the team doctor. He said it was because he was a gynecologist. *Photo courtesy of the Detroit Lions*

28

OWNERS' TRAVAILS

BROADCAST LEGACY

Even though I worked for WJR radio, covering the Lions games on the air as a color commentator from 1983-1988 (and in 1997 for WXYT), I hadn't realized that perhaps the reason WJR was the home of Lions radio was that the team's first owner just happened to own the station.

While most from the group who brought the Lions to Detroit from Portsmouth, Ohio, in 1934 were car people, executives in automobile or related businesses, principal owner, George A. "Dick" Richards, owned radio station WCX—which became WJR.

Mark Beltaire, retired columnist from the *Free Press* writing in the 1980s for *Sports Fans' Journal*, said Richards bought his tiny radio station from E.D. Stair, then owner of the *Free Press*. Stair was "a man who was Richards's equal in bullheadedness and ability to hate," Beltaire said. "They disliked each other intensely."

Then Beltaire related a tale from H.G. Salsinger, the sports editor of *The News* in those early Lions days. Salsinger said he and Richards once entered the Book Cadillac Hotel to attend some affair when a paperboy came in hawking the *Free Press*. Richards grabbed all the papers and tore them to shreds and jumped up and down on them before handing the boy $5. When Salsinger asked why he had done that, Richards responded: "Because I hate that blankety-blank Stair so much."

WCX became WJR, the jewel of Richards's empire, located in "the golden tower" of the Fisher Building. One summer day he walked into the executive offices and spied a hat on a table (one of his pet peeves). He sailed it out the window. That prompted the hat's owner—who was just about to sign a sizeable contract with the station for airtime—to glare at him and stalk away.

CEO=CANDID EXECUTIVE OWNER

William Clay Ford, owner and chairman of the Lions, always has been a very nice person and treated us with respect. As far as owners go, there's not a better one. He didn't meddle with the team, but he did, after all, have the right to be upset when things weren't going well. When that happened, look out. He wasn't one to pull punches with criticism, which usually was well deserved.

He is the last surviving grandson of auto-making pioneer Henry Ford and first got involved with the team more than a decade before I became a Lion. In October 1956 he was named to the 15-member Lions board. He was just 31 and a vice president of Ford Motor Company. Mr. Ford didn't own any Lions stock at the time. In 1964 he became sole owner of the team, buying out the other stockholders for $4.5 million. In less than two decades the Lions' estimated value ballooned to $40-$50 million.

For more than 40 years, Mr. Ford has dealt with mostly underachieving teams and without a championship to show for his dollar investment and management and numerous coaching changes. Yet throughout that time he has not shied away from the news media, being candid when asked a direct question. Perhaps the first significant indication of that came in a speech at the Grosse Pointe War Memorial in February 1965, broadcast on WWJ radio. He said the recently departed George Wilson and his staff didn't instill a winning attitude.

Wrote Ben Dunn in *The News*, "The Lions owner probably made his PR guy, Bud Erickson, wince, because in one night he expended information which, if spread out, would keep the club in the public eye from now to the opening of training camp in July." Wilson responded later by saying Ford "doesn't know the first thing about coaching football.... All I know is I'm sure happy to be out of Detroit and with the Redskins."

A headline above a letter to the editor in the September 8, 1966, *News* read, 'Ford Blamed for Lions Plight'. It was a theme that then and for decades would show up in letters and newspaper columns. Despite often taking the brunt of anger from fans for the years of mediocrity, it wasn't difficult for reporters to approach him after a bad game. They were almost assured of getting a good quote or two.

Mr. Ford was his candid self after a 24-10 loss at Minnesota on October 5, 1968, telling the press: "How can they take a day off and get away with it? They're getting paid. I've seen college players that'll give it a harder fight than that. I don't blame the staff, I blame the players, collectively."

Here are some more examples:
After a 20-20 tie against New Orleans in 1968, Mr. Ford likened the Lions to a four-engine plane sputtering along with only three engines working "and two of those are on fire."

In the 1971 preseason, following the Lions' third loss in five games, an angry Mr. Ford said: "They're just too overconfident and resting on last year's reputation. They are not sharp, not even trying. I'm very disappointed. This was a shoddy performance. There is no desire. I don't care if it's a preseason game or a Super Bowl game, we have to win them all."

In October 1973, after Detroit lost to a lousy Baltimore Colts squad, he said of the Lions: "They don't have any pride." Of the verbal lashing he gave them he said: "I hope they get mad at me to prove a point. I hope they get mad at me every week to prove a point. Nothing would make me happier." (The next week they shut out Green Bay 34-0.)

A month later, after the Lions lost 20-0 to Washington, Mr. Ford said: "They just stand around and qualify for the pension plan. Talk about a players' strike—it might be a blessing. We should vote for it." And he added that the Lions in the nationally televised game "had the distinction of disgracing themselves from coast to coast today instead of just locally."

Mr. Ford retired from the car company's board in May 2005 after almost 56 years, being first elected to it in 1948 shortly before graduating from Yale University. His son is William Clay Ford Jr., vice-chairman of the Lions and chairman and CEO of Ford Motor Company.

29

'PAPER LION'

LIONS WATCH LION MOVIE

Paper Lion was one of the first movies we saw as a team. My rookie year, the night before a game we watched the movie downtown in an area of the theater that was set aside for us. There was some decent acting on the part of Alex Karras. The other Lions players pushed themselves and you could see they weren't as comfortable with their roles as Alex was.

That movie was funny in the sense that football players were trying to become actors, and at that point you realize how difficult it is to become an actor. The movie drew a lot of attention because of the football players and George Plimpton, who was played by Alan Alda, was out there as a player. But it sure wasn't a movie that would deserve any Academy Awards. However, anyone who watched it had to be inspired by the game of football.

PARTY KICKS OFF PUBLICITY

Plimpton's book, *Paper Lion*, brought the team loads of publicity in the mid-1960s. It detailed his trial with the Lions in 1963 (and for a couple years gave sports writers the gift of a synonym for the mostly toothless Lions teams of the period). Fifteen months later there was a big party in New York City at Luchow's restaurant to announce that the book was being made into a movie. Among those at the party were Lions officials Russ Thomas, Lyall Smith, Elliott Trumbull, Sonny Grandelius, plus players Alex Karras, John Gordy, and Carl Brettschneider.

In October 1966 the *Free Press* began running excerpts from the book, but soon after announcement of the movie, publications all over, especially in Florida where the movie would be filmed starting February 5, 1968, were clamoring for information. The location site was St. Andrews Boys School in Boca Raton, Florida.

Tommy Fitzgerald of the *Miami News* wrote that the book was made possible by Miami Dolphins coach George Wilson because, when he was the Lions coach, he gave Plimpton permission to try out in 1963 as a "last string" quarterback.

Eighteen Dolphins were used as extras in the movie to augment the Lions' 30 players and staff being utilized during the six-week production. "This is not a typical, routine Hollywood football movie—a synthetic plot and the rest phony," producer Stuart Miller said in the Fitzgerald column. "Today's audiences are more sophisticated." Three or four palm trees had to be removed and replanted later. Except for the trees, St. Andrews' facility looked similar to the Lions' real training campsite at Cranbrook School outside Detroit.

'BEST LAST-STRING QB'

Alan Alda, who starred as Plimpton, had played little football, wrote Wendy Rogers of the *Miami Herald*. "My mother got the orthodontist to say football was bad for my braces... so I stopped," Alda told Rogers. He spent the previous summer practicing in front of his house in New Jersey. "I tried to rush an eight-year-old quarterback and his father hit me in the larynx," he said. "I couldn't talk for two weeks." A week later Miller called him in to test for the lead role. "Miller asked me if I played football and I say, 'Oh, yeah.'"

No one in the film wore makeup, Rogers wrote, "but every now and then a lounging Lion would yell, 'Coppertone, over here... Hey, Sea 'N Ski... Something.'" The plays being run for the camera probably were "like slow motion" to the real players, Alda said, "but it's like an express train to an amateur about to be tackled. I can guess what it would be like if they were mad at me.... I have the greatest respect for those men, and I'm being the best last-string quarterback I know how to be." Plimpton had a one-line part in the movie as team owner William Clay Ford.

FARR THE CAMERAMAN

Near the end of the filming, the *National Observer* published a feature that added more detail. Reporter Bruce Cook said a camera was strapped to the helmet of running back Mel Farr to film some of the action shots. "We're working from a straight script—and a very good one—but I think the Lions have yet to do a line exactly as it has been written," Alda was quoted as saying. That, wrote Cook, "has left screenwriter Larry Roman tearing his hair."

Lions made $350 to $1,500 a week for their work, reported sports editor Pat Harmon of the *Cincinnati Post* and *Times-Star*. And, he said somewhat prophetically, that Alex Karras "told me he may have a future in the movies. The producer liked his work so much he arranged a screen test. Alex has been offered a part in a film to be made in Italy." Karras told him in the proposed film, "I'm a character actor—comedy character."

Alex Karras was among the featured Lions from the movie *Paper Lion* here with wife, Joan, attending the world premiere of the film in Detroit.
Photo courtesy of the Detroit Lions

WORLD PREMIERE

The world premiere engagement of *Paper Lion* was at the Adams Theater in downtown Detroit in October 1968. Eleanor Breitmeyer, *The News'* society writer, covered the festivities, which included a couple Kleig lights out front and the 100-piece Royal Oak Kimball High School band. There were 44 cheerleaders from Detroit high schools (Denby, Cooley, Finney) and eight police officers on hand.

30

PAYING THE BILLS

INFLATION GALORE

Just as with anything today, we can't seem to get over how costs have skyrocketed over the years, from cars to houses, to food—and for NFL football owners. Today each player gets $120 a day in meal money alone. That per diem would have been a good day's overall pay per game for the early Lions.

When I played in the 1970s, we got $25 in meal money. Now take a look at what the players got in their 1952 championship season. A December 26, 1952, memo from Lions GM Nick Kerbawy to the players detailed the itinerary of a three-day trip to Cleveland to play the Browns. Attached was an envelope of meal money—"$7.50 to cover the cost of meals not eaten together." The allotment for breakfast was $1.50; lunch $2; dinner $2.50; plus another breakfast for $1.50.

BREAKING EVEN

The Lions are a privately held company and we're not privy to its expenses and profits, but Detroit's new NFL franchise in 1934 didn't equivocate with reporters about what it would take for the team to break even at the box office. In an October 14 article in *The Detroit News* by Harry Leduc, to make a profit the team needed to take in $8,000 a game by drawing between 8,000 and 10,000 fans. The club's payroll each game was $2,200. It cost the team $100 a game for officials and $400 a game to rent UD Stadium. Visiting teams were guaranteed $4,000. Advertising and other expenses totaled $800.

BILLS, BILLS, BILLS

Today's star NFL players may make millions of dollars, and team owners spend multimillions per season, but are they aware of what it cost 65 years ago? Sports writer Doc Holst of the *Free Press* outlined it all in an article September 20, 1940, with information supplied by Lions publicity man Tommy Emmet:

It cost the Lions $15,000 every home game to break even. And for the 11-game overall schedule, owner Fred Mandel's costs totaled $164,445. The team had 33 players, and it cost $130 each for uniforms and equipment, or $4,290. In training camp there were 44 players, there for 28 days, getting paid an average of $10 a day for a $12,320 total.

Salaries for all players for the season totaled $88,000. Medical and dental care accounted for $1,500; office expenses $13,260; plus $1,000 to sign players in the off-season; and $3,300 to pay half salary for a couple players sent to the Lions' Long Island Indians farm team. The salaries for coaches, equipment manager, ticket sellers, stadium guards, public address announcers, plus blanket and uniform cleaning, came to $25,325.

Visiting teams were guaranteed $5,000 up to a maximum of $15,000 and 40 percent after that. It also cost $10,000 over the season "to entertain celebrities." Bus rides to and from the stadium cost $150, and the team was charged $800 to use the practice field. Additionally, $1,500 was used to transport players to and from their homes at the start or end of the season.

FIRST PROFIT

The Lions reported their first ever profit after the 1951 season, a 7-4-1 campaign that put them second to the Los Angeles Rams' 8-4 mark in the Western Division. The team said it made $65,000 (despite having to pay $30,000 to Bo McMillin, the coach who was fired after the 1950 season with two years left on his contract. McMillin died of a heart attack March 31, 1952, at the age of 57.)

However, Edwin J. Anderson, who headed the syndicate that bought the club in 1948, said losses over the previous three seasons totaled $221,000, and "We're not yet out of the woods." The franchise had spent $2.75 million over four years. Owners turned down a $250,000 offer for the team from the Dallas Rangers/Texans, a team that finished 1-11 in 1952 before moving to Baltimore.

It was 1954, seven years after the purchase, that the 125 Lions stockholders, earned their first dividend—$14 a share. After the squad's 1957 championship, the Lions turned a profit of $151,052 (almost as much as it cost Fred Mandel for all expenses in the 1940 season). It was the fourth consecutive profitable season.

31

POLITICS

LONG DISTANCE TO VOTING BOOTH

We can't escape politics, but for some Lions, their interest went above and beyond the routine. Take Kelvin Pritchett, for instance. The defensive tackle, who served two stints with us, spent a bundle in the 2004 presidential election just to vote—and I admire him for it.

He played for the Jacksonville Jaguars in 1995-1998 and still was registered to vote in Florida but not in Michigan. He planned to vote by absentee ballot but didn't get it in time, so he flew to Jacksonville the day before the election, stayed overnight in a hotel, and cast his ballot on Tuesday morning, then flew back to Detroit in the afternoon.

Pritchett, whose salary was $785,600, estimated the trip cost him about $1,200. "I feel like it's just my duty as a man, as a black man, to do the right thing, and that's to vote," he said.

STUMP'N IN THE TRAINER'S ROOM

You might hear a little talk about politics here and there in the Lions locker room, but nothing like it was in Abe Kushner's trainer's room in 1940 at the Hotel Savarine, where quite often there were political debates going on between Whizzer White, the star running back and Rhodes Scholar (and future Associate Justice of the U.S. Supreme Court), and guard John Wiethe, who was running for state assembly in Ohio. (Both were named All-Pro that season.) In the spring of 1941, Wiethe joined a law firm in his hometown of Cincinnati.

Once during some of the political repartee, wrote Edgar Hayes of the *Times*, Clare Randolph heckled coach Potsy Clark for saying if a certain candidate won the election Clark would buy a farm and quit coaching. Sure enough, the candidate

Guard John Wiethe, shown here, used to debate politics with running back Whizzer White in the trainer's room. *Photo courtesy of the Detroit Lions*

won, and players gathered the next day to laughingly say goodbye to their coach—who, undoubtedly to no one's surprise—decided to stay.

REP LARY

One of our team's greatest stars, Yale Lary, became a member of the Texas state legislature in 1960, winning a runoff against the incumbent by 1,300 votes to become state representative from Tarrant County, which consisted of 450,000 people and included the city of Fort Worth. "I had to win," Lary said. "If I'd lost the election I'd never have dared show up for Detroit's opening game." He ran as a Democrat. "There are three kinds of Democrats in Texas," he said, "and no kinds of Republicans."

IF EVER THERE WAS A WHIZ THAT WAS

I was a high school student in North Carolina in the early 1960s and then a college student at the University of Minnesota during the height of the Civil Rights marches. Little did I realize then that the man president John F. Kennedy chose to oversee the federal marshals at Montgomery, Alabama, when the Freedom Riders were there was a Detroit Lions legend—Byron "Whizzer" White.

In March 1962, Kennedy named White to the U.S. Supreme Court. (The only player I knew who became a judge was Alan Page, the great defensive tackle for the Vikings.) *The News* published a feature January 31 on the appointment of White and quoted his former coach, Potsy Clark: "If Whizzer White was a street cleaner he'd be the best damned street cleaner in the business. No matter what he does, he'll be a success at it."

In World War II, White worked behind Japanese lines in the Solomon Islands while an intelligence officer in the Navy in 1943. That is when Kennedy returned to his Pacific base after a Japanese destroyer rammed his PT 109 boat. Right after the war, White headed the national Volunteers for Kennedy. He became a clerk for Chief Justice Fred Vinson.

Supreme Court Justice Byron 'Whizzer' White, the ex-Lions star, was a speaker at the dedication of the Matthai Building at Wayne State University in 1967.
Photo courtesy of the Detroit Lions

32

PRACTICAL JOKES

CLOWNING WITH COSELL

One of the greatest Lions jokes I ever saw was played on Howard Cosell in Tiger Stadium. Howard, who was one of the *Monday Night Football* TV broadcasters, loved to be the center of attention wherever he was. There was a standard trick players would pull in which someone would make a call to a house phone and the ear piece on the receiver would be covered with shaving cream. When the unsuspecting person picked up the phone and put it to his ear, he'd have an ear covered with shaving cream. I had that stunt pulled on me before.

We did that to Howard after one of the games. We knew he had a toupee and wondered how he was going to get the shaving cream out of his toupee without exposing his head. I believe to this day that it was either Alex Karras or Mike Lucci who pulled the trick on him. Someone pulled the same trick on me once at training camp at Cranbrook.

PHONY PHOTO

Karras probably was the biggest prankster. In my rookie year I didn't know what to expect. You heard of guys like Karras and Wayne Walker. Alex had gotten in this big brawl down at the Lindell A.C. (the sports bar downtown) with Dick the Bruiser, so he had this mean mentality, this reputation, that told you not to mess with him.

I remember being on the bus at our first away game when I was a rookie. If the veterans didn't accept you, you'd know it. The closer you got to sit to them, the more they accepted you. I was halfway to the back. All the veterans sat in the back. Someone tapped me on the shoulder. They passed up this photo. They said this is Alex Karras's family. So I looked and there was a picture of a normal looking boy. I flipped to the next photo and there's a normal looking girl. Then I flipped to the next picture and it's supposed to be his wife, but it's a picture of the ugliest female I've ever seen in my life.

So I'm sitting there and don't know what to do. Do I laugh? Do I tell the truth? All I could say was, "You have a nice family," and they started laughing. If you don't say the right thing, you have this monster of a defensive tackle jumping all over you as a rookie. Karras was constantly doing stuff like that, and I think to this day that is probably what made him the kind of actor he became in Hollywood.

SCHOOL SONGS

In training camp all rookies had to go through a certain amount of hazing. Making them sing their school song at mealtime was a common demand when we worked out at Cranbrook. I think my first step toward being accepted came when offensive tackle Roger Shoals (1965-1970) demanded that I sing my school song. Shoals projected himself as being a tough guy. I didn't know my school song. If you didn't know it, you'd just get up there and make up some stuff.

They knew I didn't know it, so Shoals said, "Rookie, by tomorrow night you'd better know your school song or make one up." I was intimidated and so that night I sat up most of the night making up a song and I made it about him. When I sang it the next day, the veterans ripped him and laughed at him because it was so funny. The veterans accepted me, but of course then Shoals was ticked at me, although deep down he really wasn't.

POCKET SURPRISE

Earl McCullouch was afraid of spiders and bugs of all sorts, and other things, and everybody knew it. Once one of the players took a dead bird and put it in his pocket on top of his car keys. Earl reached in to get his keys and came out with a dead bird. Talk about a kid running around the locker room having a fit.

SHOES SWIPED

Back in the days when players only had one pair of football shoes, there was a time when someone took Bill Triplett's shoes and tied them up on the flagpole. He couldn't find his shoes for practice and had to borrow a pair. Later he looked up at the flagpole and saw his shoes. Very few people knew Triplett was a part-time police officer and had a permit to carry a gun. He threatened to kill whoever tied up his shoes and to this day I don't think anybody ever told him who did it.

Faux Harassment

One of my friends was Errol Mann, the kicker. We hung out together and he still calls me. He was a character. I moved into this exclusive area of Rochester Hills, around Orion and Dutton. It was a big home and I was the first black, if not in Rochester Hills, at least in that subdivision. We were out at a little pub Errol and I used to hit. He was driving me home that night. The next night he was at the pub and I drove home. He came by later in his Jeep and was circling my house with the lights shining right into the living room. I saw the Jeep and knew who it was. The next thing I knew, here were the police coming by. The neighbors thought I was being harassed by the Ku Klux Klan or something.

We called Mann "Jack Daniels" because he loved to drink Jack Daniels whiskey. If he'd go out to practice and began missing field goals, coach Joe Schmidt would say, "You've got to hit the bar tonight." It was well known that if Errol didn't have a few his accuracy wasn't as good as it should have been.

Bang-up Stunt

Mann had a habit of sleeping with his window open in training camp. It so happened we noticed he didn't have a screen, so we got our hand on a bunch of firecrackers. He was on the second floor and there was a tree outside and we climbed up the tree and lit the firecrackers, which were all mangled together, about 50-75 of them. As they went off, we had someone on the other side of the door tie the knob to another knob across the hall so Errol couldn't open the door. We just listened as he screamed and yelled as the firecrackers went off in his room.

Spook'd

We had this thing called "The Creeper" we used to pull on the rookies in training camp. About two o'clock in the morning we'd go around to the rookies' rooms wearing a mask. We'd have a passkey and would open their door and stand over them with a flashlight shining on the mask. It was horrible. We'd shake the player until he woke up. Rockne Freitas was so surprised he broke his toe. One guy peed on himself. One guy ran into the closet and cried. When Freitas broke his toe, I think that's when Joe Schmidt said that's it, no more Creeper. We had players coming out with guns and knives.

'Important' Message

One of the stories about coaches that come to mind while I was on the staff involves Herb Patera, who was an assistant from 1989-1995. He was a former teammate of coach Wayne Fontes and was a very gullible person. You could tell him anything. He always talked about being a head coach and one day I got the idea that I would play this trick on him.

It was about the time the Atlanta Falcons announced they were going to fire their head coach, so I went to the receptionist and had her write up a little message to Herb from the owner of the Falcons and "signed" by him. The message said the Falcons were interested in interviewing him for the head coaching job and would he give the owner a call.

We were having meetings that morning. After I got the information I took it down to the defensive meeting where Wayne and Herb were sitting in. I gave Herb the message. Of course, Wayne was in on it. Herb went outside and read the message. He told Wayne he was going to be the coach of the Atlanta Falcons.

He went up to his office and placed the phone call and asked for the owner and that he wanted to set up an appointment for the interview. The owner told the girl he didn't know who Herb was, and he definitely was not one of the candidates for the job.

LUCK TURNER

We lost the season opener in 1984 at home to San Francisco, 30-27. After the game, trainer Kent Falb used his hand and broke a mirror. We had made the playoffs in 1983, but didn't make it again until 1991—the proverbial seven years of bad luck. We played at San Francisco in 1991 (losing there 15-3) and the first thing we did was to tape over all the mirrors.

FRIDAY'S 'MONGOOSE'

Practical jokes were a staple with players long before I came into the game and, as far as the Lions go, I wouldn't be surprised if a lot of that began with our equipment man, Friday Macklem, whose history with the team goes back to 1936. He used to play this trick on the players with a "pet mongoose." It was some furry gadget in a wooden box and when someone opened it, it would pop out. A lot of the effect came from the set-up to the gag, telling rookies not to look into it or to be careful when they did. I've seen guys actually wet themselves as a result of that joke.

MONEY LESSON FROM 'LITTLE CHRIS'

Macklem was around when the following story from Edgar Hayes of the *Detroit Times* hit the paper in May 1940, but Macklem didn't have anything to do with this one. It was a humorous lesson that Frank "Little Chris" Christensen taught his brother, George "Big Chris" Christensen, and their friend, Vern Huffman. Frank, a

George Christensen, shown here, had to learn a lesson from his younger brother Frank regarding their respective monetary value to the Lions.
Photo courtesy of the Detroit Lions

two-way back, and George, a tackle, were Lions teammates from 1934-1937. George was still with the team in 1938, as was back Huffman.

It seems that Frank was injured early in the season of his final year with Detroit, 1937, and consequently benched. Huffman then took over Frank's blocking back position, and then George was slowly converted to being a blocking back, too. One payday, Hayes related, the three of them were talking about their paychecks. Huffman and "Big Chris" suspected "Little Chris" was making a lot more money than they were and they enticed him into a deal whereby the three of them would pool their money and divide it up equally.

As it turned out, though, George and Vern had ganged up on themselves because Frank's check was only $50—about 25 percent less than they were making. Instead of taking the windfall, Frank charged them both $1 for the lesson and let them off the hook.

'LOGAN' HAD SHORT RUN

During the 1952 season, Lions players often were sent messages of encouragement. They were signed, simply, "Logan." It took a while, but eventually "Logan" was revealed to be backup quarterback Jim Hardy, a good-natured sort of fellow who played just one year for the team. When he announced the following summer that he would quit after the All-Star Game to devote more time to the plastics business in Los Angeles, of which he owned 50 percent, news stories all mentioned him as being "Logan." Tom Dublinski took over his spot as No. 2 QB in 1953.

JOCK-ULAR

Hardy also was part of another joke. Quarterback Bobby Layne, on hand to make the coin flip at Super Bowl XVI at the Silverdome, told magazine writer Mickey Herskowitz about the time Hardy rented a plane and buzzed the practice field and dropped 144 jockstraps on his teammates.

GREEN JOCKS

Layne told another story to Herskowitz, this one involving the players' wives at the NFL title game in 1953. "Chlorophyll was real big that year," Layne said. "You had it in toothpaste, chewing gum, everything. So we had a slogan: 'Chlorophyll will put more sock in your jock.' The day we beat Cleveland in the championship game, all our wives sat up there in the stands wearing hats that they'd made from jockstraps dyed green. Some tied a bow in 'em, some of them wore them as a band... and it was pretty cute."

33

PUBLICITY: STUNTS AND MORE

NFL team public relations directors don't need to concoct off-the-wall gimmicks to get publicity nowadays. Actually, often they need to find ways to diffuse publicity caused by egocentric players or ones who get into trouble with the law. But when the Lions were just getting off the ground, anything that might garner some free ink in the newspapers, or free airtime on radio, was welcomed.

CHIMP 'SIGNS'

Veteran Detroiters remember the famous chimpanzee at the Detroit Zoo named Jo Mendi. Well, how many remember that Mendi was "signed" by the Detroit Lions in August 1934? The team obviously wasn't averse to such publicity stunts, being new to the city that year.

All the newspapers carried stories of the signing and one of them, the *Detroit Times*, even carried a column "By Jo Mendi, as told to Edgar Hayes." The *Detroit News* ran three photos of him in uniform, with the jersey number "0." According to the *Free Press*, the Lions signed the chimp as "a roving center on defense and to handle the forward passing on attack."

In training camp, coach Potsy Clark said of Mendi: "He looks like good material, but he needs discipline. We don't want any prima donnas on this ball club." In "his" *Times* column, the chimp said: "I'll play any position just as long as I can get away from those sissy games, skipping rope and roller skating."

MOVIE STARS AT GAMES

It wasn't only when the NFL expanded to southern California that movie stars could be seen at Lions games. In 1935 when the Lions won the championship, among those in the crowd (and who wound up with his picture splashed in the papers) was comedian Joe E. Brown, who had also been to Detroit a few months earlier to watch the Tigers win the World Series.

Another star visit that got plenty of ink was when Jane Russell, the buxom Hollywood sex symbol of that era, attended a Lions game in October 1949 when they played the Rams. Her husband was quarterback Bob Waterfield of the newly transplanted Los Angeles team, which used to be in Cleveland. Also quarterbacking that team was Norm Van Brocklin. The Lions lost 21-10.

DUTCH JR. SIGNED... AT AGE THREE

Perhaps the "signing" of chimp Jo Mendi from the zoo was a measure of publicity stunts to come for the young Lions. Two years later, in September 1936, the team "signed" quarterback Dutch Clark's three-year-old son, Earl Jr., to a "contract."

"Not to be outdone by the Detroit Tigers, who have signed 11-year-old quadruplets from Beaumont, Texas, the Detroit Lions pro football team has signed the three-year-old son of Earl 'Dutch' Clark, ace backfield performer of the National League squad," said the *Flint Journal*. "Terms specify that the youngster gets $500 a game if he makes the team along about 1956."

HANKY WAVERS?

The Lions have worn "Honolulu blue" and silver uniforms since they debuted in Detroit for owner G.A. Richards. They had played an exhibition game in Hawaii, and Richards designed the uniforms especially for the occasion.

Mark Beltaire, in his February 1988 column in *Sports Fans' Journal,* said that even Tommy Emmet, the Lions' publicist extraordinaire, couldn't go along with a suggestion from Richards that the players be provided with blue handkerchiefs so they could back off the field after a game with little dance steps, waving aloha to the crowd.

BATTLE FOR JOBS

Back in 1938, just like today, Lions fans were very interested in whether their favorite newcomers, be they draftees, free agents, or those acquired in trade, would make the team after the final cuts of training camp. Always cognizant of a chance to make a little money, the Lions touted a preseason scrimmage between the newcomers and veterans as the "Annual Battle for Jobs." The 1938 battle, "Lions Freshmen vs. Varsity," newspaper ads declared, was held on a Friday at 7:30 p.m. at UD Stadium. Tickets cost 50 cents.

The following week they opened the season at Briggs Stadium against the Pittsburgh Pirates, and their ads, instead of centering on their debut in the newly expanded home of baseball's Tigers, billed the game as "Dutch Clark vs. Whizzer White."

TECHNICAL ASSISTANCE

The NFL's official movie produced after the 1938 season was called *Champions of the Gridiron*, and coach Dutch Clark of the Lions was the technical supervisor, with assistance from his coaching staff. Clark displayed techniques using the football talents of various league players, including Whizzer White (not yet a Lion), Sammy Baugh, Bill Hewitt, and Jack Manders. Industrial Pictures Inc. of Detroit produced the film for General Mills, and Lions announcer Harry Wismer narrated it.

'LIONS' LOPE'

A photo in the *Detroit Times* in the fall of 1940 showed Lions quarterback Cotton Price dancing at the Arthur Murray Studio with teachers Don Davison and Sally Stritch. They were doing the "Lions' Lope." (The studio was on Washington Boulevard and Michigan Avenue. Some years later two of the teachers there were Anne and Helen Sabo, sisters of *Free Press* sports writer John N. Sabo.)

TOUR OF HOLLYWOOD

AP Newsfeatures service sent out a six-picture feature about tennis star Nancy Chaffee taking Bobby Layne and Doak Walker on a tour of Hollywood when the Lions stars were in Los Angeles in 1950 for a game against the Rams. The players and Chaffee, who won the national women's indoor championship that year, were shown visiting the famous Brown Derby restaurant and Walker putting his feet in Joe E. Brown's footprints at Grauman's Chinese Theatre.

MEAN MASCOT

Shrine Circus came to town in March 1951 and one of the lions of famous animal trainer Clyde Beatty mauled a tiger from the show. The Detroit Lions board of directors briefly considered an offer of whether to accept the lion as the team's mascot.

COACHING CLINIC

In August 1952, the *Detroit Courier* newspaper, which was published for the African-American community, held its second annual coaching clinic, and Coach Buddy Parker of the Lions was among the guests. Others included basketball's Bob

Calihan from UD, and high school coach and *Courier* columnist Will Robinson, and manager Fred Hutchinson of the Detroit Tigers.

WATER BOY CONTEST

Being a team water boy used to be quite a special honor, like being bat boy in baseball, and the *Free Press* ran a contest early in the 1952 season that required each entrant to write a 150-work essay on "Why I would like to be the Lions water boy." The winner would get to work at the upcoming home game against San Francisco and then go with his dad to Chicago for the Bears game. The contest was for Detroit schoolboys aged 12-17.

GIVING UP HIS SEAT

In the summer of 1953 the Lions (who had gotten bad publicity recently due to some barroom tussles) got some good ink when owner Edwin J. Anderson and general manager Nick Kerbawy were on a plane at the Traverse City airport in northern Michigan and the captain asked for a volunteer to get off. A 10-year-old boy needed the seat to fly to Detroit for an appendectomy. The two Lions executives flipped a coin and Kerbawy lost and headed out the door. "Wait a minute," Anderson shouted. "I won, didn't I? I want to get off the plane—for that boy."

INSIDE LOOK AT HAZING

Today they might keep the press out, but in August 1954 the Lions didn't mind the publicity, and so *The News* sent a photographer to the team's training camp "rookie night" and the paper ran a funny photo showing tackles Gerry Perry and Ray Westort, plus halfback Gene Smith, in dresses and wigs pretending to be the McGuire Sisters, a top singing group of the time.

FAB FIVE

The Beatles were just becoming popular in the U.S., and the February 14, 1964, *Free Press* decided to run a "guess who" photo feature of 10 celebrities wearing the British singing group's mop-hair style wigs. Among them were executives William Clay Ford and Edwin Anderson of the Lions. Others included governor George Romney and labor leader Walter Reuther.

34

QUARTERBACK TALES

Vince Doyle, in the April 1987 *Sports Fans' Journal*, quoted 1950s superstar end Leon Hart as saying a quarterback is the worst player on the field: "He can't tackle. He can't block. Most of 'em can't run. And the coach has to do the thinking for them and call the plays." The Lions have had countless quarterbacks over the years, some have been mentioned elsewhere among these tales. But here are a few more:

'CORNER' BACK

Greg Landry (1968-1978) and I were contemporaries. He was the Lions' No. 1 draft choice in 1968 and the first quarterback taken overall. That was the year I was drafted on the third round. In 1969, an AP story joked that he might soon be a "cornerback"—because he was going back to a roomier corner spot in the Tiger Stadium locker room because of all the attention he was getting. Quarterbacks always have lots of reporters around their cubicle after a game, win or lose, but since the 22-year-old Landry was only in his second year, he didn't merit a corner locker. Those typically went to stars and distinguished veterans.

Early in the 1969 season, starting quarterback Bill Munson was injured, and Landry, the team's No. 1 draft choice from Massachusetts a year earlier, had to take over. He helped lead Detroit to a 27-21 victory at home over the Atlanta Falcons on November 9, raising his record to 3-1 in relief of Munson. With reporters jostling for position around his cubicle in the middle of the 57-year-old, cramped home team locker room, one teammate had a tough time squeezing by to get to his locker. "Greg, you're going to get moved," he said. "One more week and you're going to the corner."

Landry displayed a confidence that wasn't egocentric, and it was a sign that the Lions had indeed gotten a good selection in that 1968 draft. "I'm 3-1 for four games, and I feel good about it," Landry said. "But not about my performance, about the performance of everybody."

After playing together on the college team in the College All-Star game in 1968, Greg and I rode back to Detroit in my new car that I bought with my bonus. He was talking about business and I said, "Why are we riding in my car and you're the one who has all the money?" To this day I always kid him that he always has so much money because he doesn't spend it.

BAD LUCK TO THE END

Bill Munson (1968-1976) had so much going for him—except luck. The quarterback with the square-jawed Hollywood good looks (his nickname was "Chisel"), plus personality and playing ability to match, seemed a good fit for the Los Angeles Rams. And, in fact, it was the Rams who picked the Utah State star as their first draft choice in 1964 and made him their starter as a rookie.

But bad luck soon struck. A knee injury and subsequent operation in 1965 knocked Munson from the starter's role. In 1968 he was traded to the Lions in a blockbuster deal that sent QB Milt Plum, running back Tommy Watkins, and wide receiver Pat Studstill to the Rams. As popular as those players were, Munson didn't give distraught Lions fans an opportunity to complain, setting an all-time team record for completions in a season with 181 that year.

Then, early in the 1969 season, Munson got hurt again, and it gave an opportunity to a second-year man who happened to be the Lions' No. 1 draft pick a year earlier, Greg Landry, who then emerged as the top signal caller. Munson held out in his contract negotiations in the summer of 1972, then reluctantly gave in and in July signed general manager Russ Thomas's offer of a four-year deal. That proved to be a bit of more bad luck because the next day Roman Gabriel, the Rams' quarterback, suffered a collapsed lung and was hospitalized. Having been an ex-Ram with a lot of credentials would have made Munson a good candidate to be signed by Los Angeles as a free agent to fill in for Gabriel. Instead, he was locked into the Lions for four years, likely to be Landry's backup.

Munson said his agent, lawyer Ed Hookstratten of Beverly Hills, California talked him into signing. "I got in touch with him about 5 p.m. yesterday," Munson said then. "I hadn't talked to him in four or five days. He said I might as well not go on with this [holdout] any further."

Injuries continued to plague him, yet Landry, too, was the victim of numerous injuries and that put Munson back at the No. 1 spot off and on. He seemed to be going great in 1974 and even set a team record in completion percentage (56.8 percent on 166 of 292) before separating his shoulder in the 11th game, leading to another operation. In 1975, Munson injured a collarbone in preseason, and in the sixth game of the regular season he suffered another knee injury, requiring cartilage and ligament surgery.

We used to take his crutches and hide them and everyone would disappear.

Munson's final bit of bad luck happened July 10, 2000, when he drowned in the swimming pool of his home in Lodi, California. He was 58. However, he had lived in Birmingham, Michigan, for 33 years, and there were many Lions who attended his funeral there at Holy Name Roman Catholic Church.

PLUCKED FROM THE PLANT

I guess you could say I had a lot to do with Gary Danielson's Lions career (1976-1984). We had cut him and he was working in a sheet metal plant in the Detroit area. A quarterback got hurt, and coach Rick Forzano met with me as captain and I said we should bring Gary Danielson back. He had been cut in training camp. And since he was local we knew where to find him.

He had signed as a free agent in 1976. It was a good move, especially in view of the fact that during much of the 1970s the team didn't seem be very interested in local talent, be it from the University of Michigan, Michigan State, or elsewhere. Danielson was a star at Dearborn Divine Child High School, leading the Catholic League powerhouse to the state championship in 1968. He became a star quarterback at Purdue University but was passed over in the draft and played in 1974 in the World Football League.

There was something about him, though, that the Lions saw, a charisma that makes for great quarterbacks. However, after a December game in 1978 in which he threw five interceptions in a loss to St. Louis, charisma wasn't a word likely to be used about him. Yet, how quickly things changed.

A week later Danielson, who said he didn't shave for a week because of the poor performance against the Cardinals, threw for a Detroit-record five touchdown passes as the Lions crushed the usually dominant Minnesota Vikings, 45-14. Danielson completed 26 of 32 passes for 352 yards. Three of the TD passes went to wide receiver Leonard Thompson. "Gary's fantastic," Thompson said. "You've got to be cocky to be quarterback and Gary's a cocky individual. You've got to have a lot of pride and charisma and we're getting it."

Unfortunately, injuries kept Danielson out of action the entire 1979 season and much of the 1981 campaign. Sandwiched in between, though, was a 1980 season in which he set Lions marks for passing attempts (417), completions (244), yards (3,223), and completion percentage (58.5). His 11,885 passing yardage for his career is fourth all time in Detroit, and he is among the top five in a number of other categories.

It didn't take long for him to begin to find his niche in television. In his Lions days he worked locally with WDIV-TV as a sportscaster and Easter Seals Telethon host. Perhaps it was that charisma that later on helped him become one of television's top national college football game analysts.

35

RIVAL LEAGUES

WFL Entices

During my career the World Football League and U.S. Football League emerged and vanished in a short time. We knew the NFL was dominant and those leagues wouldn't break the NFL, but they proved there was some talent out there that teams missed.

I thought my big moment would be in the WFL. A few players had made the jump there. Tom Fears was the general manager of the Los Angeles team, the Southern California Sun. I had been with the Lions five or six years, but I visited them to hear their offer because they were talking big money—but they never came up with it.

All-American League Stirs Ire

With World War II winding down, the Lions of 1945, like other NFL teams, were concerned about losing players to the upstart new All-America Professional Football Conference, and also the Canadian league. Lions owner Fred Mandel was particularly vocal about it and said in an AP story in October that the AAPFC was a "propaganda league" and he "refused to be taken in by the new leagues publicity program."

He particularly was disturbed by a running fight for the post-war services of Marine Lt. Elroy "Crazylegs" Hirsch, who played his college ball at Michigan and Wisconsin. Mandel said he was "issuing a warning to boys in the service who are or might be Lion property that they think twice before accepting as fact claims of the new league receiving wide ballyhoo in the press…. The history of the new league so far is one of false claims and broken promises."

The new league purportedly signed a half-dozen Lions, four of them draftees and two who had already played with Detroit before the war, John Tripson and John

Polanski. The other four—Chuck Jacoby (Indiana), Alex Kapter, and Otto Graham (Northwestern), and Gene Fekete (Ohio State)—had college eligibility remaining. "The conference is ruining pro football's fine past relations with the colleges," Mandel said. Other Lions who left for the other league were Ed Frutig, Charles Fennebock, and Bill Radovich.

Eventually, though, the AAPFC merged with the NFL, and Detroit wound up getting outstanding players from former AAPFC teams, ones who they'd use to build their great teams of the 1950s, such as: Bobby Layne, Cloyce Box, Lou Creekmur, Bob Smith, and Bob Hoernschemeyer.

SINK-SWITCH

United Press reported out of Atlanta in December 1945 that Lions quarterback star Frank Sinkwich was retiring to devote time "to the beanery and bar" he owned in Youngstown, Ohio. Sinkwich, the former Heisman Trophy winner from Georgia, the NFL's MVP in 1944, said a knee injury suffered while playing with a 2nd Air Force team led to the decision. He had been back in the Army but was officially discharged again December 5, 1945, and said he would return to the Lions. However, five days later *The News* said Sinkwich had signed a three-year contract with the New York Yankees, the team of former NFL Brooklyn franchise owner Dan Topping in the new All-American conference. Sinkwich reportedly was going to get $12,500 a year, compared with his Lions salary of $2,500.

Fred DeLano, Detroit's public relations director, told the press: "We will go to court to keep him," claiming he had one more year to run on his contract since he didn't play in 1945.

MERGER HELPS...AND HURTS

The long-simmering feud and competition between the NFL and the young AAPFC came to a close with the merger of the leagues in December 1949. But the Lions still had concerns, particularly about losing draft rights to Leon Hart of Notre Dame and Doak Walker of Southern Methodist. Eventually, though, the Lions got them both, and they became superstar mainstays of their championship teams of the 1950s. The NFL upheld Detroit's early draft of Hart, and he became their No. 1 pick as a bonus choice in 1950.

The merger, coach Bo McMillin said in Bob Latshaw's *Free Press* story, "means that now we can be certain of the players we draft. It's going to cut down on the suicidal bidding against another team for top college stars." Lions co-captain (and later executive vice president and general manager) Russ Thomas, said, "Players' contracts will probably be smaller in the long run, but I don't think it will hit established pro players too badly."

McMillin said the stature of the pro game was now such that teams wouldn't ask guys to "play for peanuts." However, within a couple years, players who had seen their salaries slashed would go elsewhere, like to the Canadian league, for more money. In 1953, Lions began negotiating two-year contracts to try to break the salary jam.

BORDER RAIDS

There was a lot of controversy in the 1950s over Canadian teams trying to steal NFL players. The AP reported in February 1955 that the Canadian Big Four League had abandoned any effort to sign a no-raiding agreement until 1956. The CFL wasn't some upstart league. The Toronto Argonauts are the oldest sports franchise in North America. The 2004 season, which concluded with the Grey Cup championship game, was the best for attendance in 20 years, and there was talk of expansion.

A *Detroit News* story said the Lions were spending $400,000 a year in salaries in 1955. At the time, the Lions were battling with the Toronto Argonauts over tackle Gil Mains. Detroit's No. 3 draft pick, defensive end Darris McCord, was reported to be headed to Canada to play, and the Lions said they had changed the mind of Bill Stits from going there.

Pat Oleksiak, their 18th-round draft pick, was signed by Winnipeg of the Western Interprovincial League, and quarterback Tom Dublinski signed with Toronto. In September, a court in Long Beach, California, ruled in favor of an injunction that said linebacker/kicker Jim Martin couldn't leave the Lions for the Argonauts.

The Canadian league also coveted Howard "Hopalong" Cassady, the Heisman Trophy winner from Ohio State, but the Lions outbid for him. Cassady, one of the leading baseball players in the Big Ten, also considered playing that sport instead. He could have gotten a big bonus to play baseball. He was an outfielder with a good arm. Another Lion who had an eye on a baseball career was quarterback Earl Morrall of Michigan State, who was drafted by San Francisco, but played for Detroit from 1958-1964.

Dublinski jumped to Toronto in March 1955 for a reported $18,000 a year. (That was eight months after the NFL reported a peace accord in its war with the Canadian league for players.)

Competition from Canada didn't seem to wane in the early 1960s. Toronto signed Lions quarterback Tobin Rote in January 1960 for a reported $23,000, a $5,000 raise over what he was making with the Lions.

'HIPPITY' HOPS TO RIVAL

A decade before "Hopalong" Cassady played for the Lions, they had a triple-threat back named Harry "Hippity" Hopp, an All-American from Nebraska. He was with the Lions from 1940-1943 and then played on service teams while in the Navy. But in 1946 he signed with Buffalo of the AAPFC. It was the third key loss for

Detroit in three days, preceded by Whizzer White and Frank Sinkwich retiring, although Sinkwich unretired to join the rival AAPFC. White, a future Supreme Court Justice who studied at Oxford University in England in 1939 on a Rhodes scholarship, got his law degree from Yale, and in January 1947 became a Supreme Court clerk—and that was after earning two Bronze Stars in the Navy.

Even trainer "Scrap Iron" Young bolted to the other league in 1946, joining the Chicago Rockets. He was with Detroit just one year. The Lions then brought back Dr. Raymond Forsyth, their trainer in 1943-1944, and gave him an assistant, Dr. Homer Allshouse.

'WELCOME' OF NEW LEAGUE?

When the American Football League announced in 1959 that it would get underway in 1960, the *UPI* story said the NFL "welcomes" the new league. Many headlines in the days and months afterwards spoke of the NFL's plans to expand, an obvious effort to offset the emergence of the rival AFL.

The NFL's decision to expand paid off early when, in June 1960 the AFL pulled out of Minnesota and Dallas because the NFL expanded to those cities. The league said the price for an expansion team was $600,000.

36

STADIUM STORIES

SILVERDOME'S DEBUT

When we played at Tiger Stadium, I don't think we ever pictured ourselves playing out of the city. There was always talk about a possible new stadium, on the riverfront downtown or out on the State Fairgrounds property by 8 Mile Road. But soon we found ourselves playing in Pontiac Stadium out in Oakland County, and once we got adjusted to playing inside we'd win there, while other teams came in and were sucking air. There wasn't much circulation, but we practiced there and got used to it.

The dome made its debut August 23, 1975, and the Lions played there through 2001. The first event was an exhibition against the Kansas City Chiefs. We won, 27-24. Credentialed press members had to walk through the mud and enter the stadium through the kitchen of the restaurant that wasn't as yet opened in the facility.

There were a few glitches, as well, including the fact that the 10-acre Teflon-coated fiberglass roof of the first ever air-inflated domed stadium wasn't ready to inflate because some panels were missing, and the material rested on cables that hung across the top perimeter of the building. Any extra-high punts would hit the roof, which weighed some 200 tons. For events, 29 blowers were used to pump air, although at other times only two blowers were used.

One incongruity jumped out that first day: advertising blimps and airplanes flew over the stadium with banners and signs. The advertisers and air services either were unaware the stadium would be roofed, or they just figured with an 80,400-seat facility they could draw attention of fans entering and perhaps from the many TV cameras outside to record the grand opening. The $55.7 million stadium welcomed a crowd of 62,094 for the exhibition game, and some of the people got wet from rain that overflowed from the roof into the stands, also making the artificial field soggy in places.

"It's a beautiful, beautiful stadium," one fan said, when the Lions were trailing. "Too bad the team that plays in it is not as impressive, but it's better to have a nice facility and a bad team than both a bad facility and a bad team like we had in the past." Seven weeks later the Lions gave the dome another inauguration, with the first regular-season game there, a nationally televised 36-10 loss to the Dallas Cowboys. The roof was inflated for the first time four days earlier.

The first big test for the dome came November 27 in the annual Thanksgiving Day matchup, a 20-0 loss to the Los Angeles Rams that pretty much wiped out Detroit's hopes of making the playoffs. It snowed six inches before the national TV game and pumps that were supposed to channel melting snow from the roof weren't available. So workers opened vents in the dome to let the water drain, and that made the field soggy once again.

The stadium suffered a few other problems over the years, mostly weather-related, including heavy winds that ripped off some roof panels in August 1976. But the glitches were dealt with, and events went on. However, there was one problem that wasn't solved—a better deal for the Lions in their lease agreement with the city of Pontiac.

Eventually negotiations broke down, and team owner Ford decided to break the lease, make a cash settlement, and build a new stadium in Detroit—Ford Field—next to the new baseball field for the Detroit Tigers, Comerica Park. Subsequently the Lions won the bid for the 2006 Super Bowl game. Pontiac, meanwhile, was saddled with a huge stadium and the task of finding events (like tractor pulls, circuses, and trade shows) to fill it. The parking lot eventually became home to a drive-in theater.

POTENTIAL SITE

The State Fairgrounds at Woodward and Eight Mile Road on Detroit's northern border perpetually were in the news as a site for one major project or another, none of which ever came to fruition. One of them was an 85,000-seat stadium for the Lions. "If we get the stadium I hope the Tigers can move there, too," said Lions board member William Clay Ford in a *News* Q & A in January 1962. The Lions had five years to go on their lease to play at Tiger Stadium.

A Michigan House committee in Lansing in March 1963 held off on a bill to help finance a $25 million stadium until Detroit was selected to host the 1968 Summer Olympics. The state planned to raise $1.6 million through an increase in taxes from horse race bets. Detroit didn't get the Olympics.

SEND 'EM TO THE BRIGGS

Professional football was making great strides in the 1930s and it was obvious that the University of Detroit Stadium, first home of the Lions, wasn't going to accommodate the increased demand for tickets. In March 1938 the Lions announced they would move to the enlarged Briggs Stadium, home of baseball's Detroit Tigers. The Lions had no home games scheduled in September, so there were no conflicts because of Tigers games.

Briggs Stadium became the sixth major park converted to accommodate football as well as baseball. The others were Wrigley Field in Chicago, the Polo Grounds in New York, Ebbets Field in Brooklyn, Griffith Stadium in Washington, D.C., and League Park in Cleveland. The debut game at Briggs was September 9, 1938, when the Lions beat Pittsburgh 16-7.

The gridiron at Briggs was laid out with its west sideline at a right angle to second base on the baseball infield and ran parallel to the third base line. The west sideline was 75 feet from the Tigers dugout, and the east sideline was 100 feet from the right field stands. More than 2,300 yards of sod were used to cover the base paths. They were rolled with a 4,000-pound roller that was so effective that by early October the sod already had taken root.

The Lions weren't Detroit's first pro football team to play in Briggs Stadium. In the mid-1920s, Jim Conzelman's Detroit Panthers played in Navin Field (later called Briggs, then Tiger, Stadium).

"We wouldn't let them run their football field across the diamond. We didn't want them to spoil the infield paths," said Neil Conway, veteran Tigers groundskeeper, quoted in an October 12, 1938, *Detroit News* article. "But now the southwest corner of the new Lion gridiron completely covers the diamond."

Briggs Stadium was the home of the Lions for many years until they moved to the dome in Pontiac in 1975. This is a game in 1946. *Photo courtesy of the Detroit Lions*

Stadium Snit

There were recalcitrant board members and deteriorating player talent when Chicagoan Fred Mandel bought the Lions in 1940, and he would get indications of worse news—that Walter Briggs, owner of the Detroit Tigers, might not want the Lions to play at Briggs Stadium anymore.

Briggs wasn't angry at the new management, said his son, Spike Briggs, in a *Free Press* column by Charles P. Ward, but "Dad just didn't like the looks of our field late last summer, and he wondered whether the football team was responsible for the bumpiness. He is going to postpone a decision on the Lions until next summer. He is going to take a look at the field in June, July, or August, and if it is bumpy the Lions are out. Briggs Stadium is a baseball park."

In August, Walter Briggs belatedly offered the stadium to the Lions again, but Mandel declined, saying he already had worked out a deal to go back to the University of Detroit Stadium.

Sports columnist John N. Sabo of the *Free Press* wondered aloud: "Would Fred Mandel have bought the Detroit Lions if he had known that Briggs Stadium would not be available?" Sabo also wrote that Reverend James Martin, athletic director at Catholic Central High School, was worried that his school's big game against Hamtramck at Keyworth Stadium might be sparsely attended because the Lions opened the same day at UD against Pittsburgh, and the Tigers were home against Cleveland. Because of such situations, Sabo wrote, "don't be surprised if some Catholic League games" would be played on Sunday nights at Mack Park.

In 1941, the Lions returned to Briggs Stadium after the Tigers had installed a drainage and sprinkler system to improve the field for baseball. That move pretty much wiped out the chance that a team from the rival American Professional Football League would establish a franchise in Detroit, which was one of five cities with representatives who were approached about having a team. (A couple weeks later, the Lions hired 42-year-old Graham P. Smith as their general manager. He was an ex-Marine from Chicago.)

Buying Briggs

In February 1957 the Lions pursued the idea of buying Briggs Stadium—and the whole Tigers baseball team—from the estate of Walter O. Briggs. The Lions were among a half-dozen groups that put up a bond of $250,000 each to examine the Tigers' books. A $4.5 million sale price was estimated. But NFL commissioner Bert Bell polled other members of the 12-team league and turned down the Lions' request to buy the baseball team.

Among others interested at the time were Bill Veeck, Charley Finley, movie producer Robert Goldstein, and actor Clark Gable, Detroit radio and TV station owner George Storer, Detroit radio station owner Fred Knorr, and Toronto publisher Jack Kent Cooke.

37

STUDENTS OF THE GAME

No Joke on the Field

Bob Kowalkowski (1966-1976) was a short, well-built guard who played for a lot of years because he was such a student of the game. When he was on the field and had that uniform on he was serious. Once he took it off he could joke and shoot the breeze with the best of 'em. His son, linebacker Scott Kowalkowski, played with the Lions from 1994-2001 and was a standout on special teams.

When Scott was a young boy, his father told me his son idolized me and didn't think his dad was as good. Scott would offer to carry my pads—but not his dad's. I had a chance to coach Scott, and he told me himself I was one of his favorite players.

Special Savvy

Dick LeBeau (CB, 1959-1972) was a very shrewd player. The funniest thing I ever saw him do came in a game when he and Tommy Vaughn, the two safeties, had a busted coverage and the other team scored a touchdown. We as offensive players, plus other players on the bench, didn't really know what happened, but we could see LeBeau run over to Tommy and start pointing his finger at him. So everyone who saw that figured it was Vaughn who blew the coverage.

Later, Tommy came over and we asked him what was going on. He said, "I don't understand it. He was in my face pointing his finger at me and kept saying, 'It was my fault. It was my fault.' I said, 'You mean it was my fault?,' and he said, no, it was his fault, but everybody was thinking it was my fault."

Father Figure

As tough as linebacker Mike Lucci (1965-1973) was on the field, in person he was the reserved fatherly type who was all business. You could tell he worked at being what he was and took it very seriously. He held the team together. He always was someone you'd listen to and go to for advice.

1970 was the first year people realized how good he was. He was always competing with Dick Butkus of the Chicago Bears as to who was the best linebacker in the NFL. When he finally made the Pro Bowl game in 1972 he got some of the recognition he deserved. Lucci was our defensive MVP in 1969, 1970, and 1971.

Survival Instinct

Linebacker Wayne Walker (1958-1972) was similar in some respects to Lucci, but not as stern. He had a kind of kid side to him, although he probably was the oldest guy on the team when I was there. Over the years I learned you had to have his approach in order to survive in the NFL for such a long time. We had a lot of respect for Walker and Lucci, not just because of their ability, but because of their longevity, too. Walker became a local TV sports anchor for a while and then went out to San Francisco to take a TV sports job out there. When he was a Lion, he was among a group of NFL players who visited our troops in Vietnam.

38

TEASER SEASON

T-E-A-M Team

The Lions of 1970 was made up primarily of older players and they really came together as a unit. If the team hadn't lost 5-0 to the Dallas Cowboys in the first round of the playoffs, I think we could have won the Super Bowl. The older guys kept the younger ones intact. One of our rituals was to always meet as a team at Larco's restaurant on Six Mile Road after a home game. Some would show up. Others wouldn't. But the older guys were there. If you didn't show up they'd get on you Monday in the meetings to let you know this was a TEAM. It was such a close-unit team. Even the coaches were there. It was just a great team to be around.

The downfall of the Lions in the 1970s, I believe, was because they never, over a reasonable period of time, replaced those older guys with good, young players. The transition wasn't gradual, but sudden, and that's why the rest of the decade saw the Lions struggle most of the time.

That 1970 team was dedicated to winning. I remember some great games that year. Not only was that a turning point for the team, but for me in terms of being an offensive factor. (I ended up as the offensive MVP for the season, with linebacker Mike Lucci the defensive MVP. Running back Mel Farr, center Ed Flanagan, linebacker Paul Naumoff, and I went to the Pro Bowl game.)

We had to play four of five division leaders the last five games of the season. The turning point was the Thanksgiving Day game at home against the Oakland Raiders. We didn't often get a chance to perform on national TV, but we did because of the annual Thanksgiving game. It was an opportunity for people to see what we were all about. I really psyched myself up for that game. We were winning 14-0 and had the ball. Mel Farr was running right and stepped out of bounds and took a late hit from defensive end Ben Davis. Both benches erupted. They were both on the same sideline. There were fisticuffs, pushing and shoving.

At that point the Detroit Lions didn't feel like they were going to be manhandled by the Black and Silver rough guys of the NFL. We went on to win that game 28-14, and I think that's when we grew up as a team, realizing we could compete with anyone. We beat St. Louis 16-3 at home the following week, then won 28-23 in Los Angeles. The weather was bad in December, but we closed out the season at Tiger Stadium by shutting out Green Bay 20-0. By winning our last five games we finished second in the National Football Conference Central Division behind Minnesota, ending up with a 10-4 regular-season record.

The playoff game was at Dallas the day after Christmas. That 5-0 loss was a crushing blow to all Lions fans and to all of us who felt we let everyone down after building their hopes so high.

I'll never forget during Christmas week of practice for the game against the Cowboys, Lions owner William Clay Ford walked around the locker room and gave every player a $100 bonus. That may not sound like much now, but that was a lot of money back then, and he gave it to us out of the goodness of his heart so we'd have some extra money to spend when we were away from home. He didn't have to do it, but he cared. It's a shame that the Lions haven't presented him with a championship by now in spite of the loyalty and dollars he has spent making the organization what it is. I hope real soon that a championship can be brought to the Ford family.

DEMPSEY'S STUNNER

One of our losses in 1970 was the stunning 19-17 defeat at New Orleans when Rick Dempsey ended the game by kicking his record-setting 63-yard field goal. He had been an erratic kicker, one who was born without a right hand and without toes on his right foot. He used a special shoe. To this day I don't think anyone on our team believes what happened to us.

We considered Dempsey to be an average field goal kicker. Nobody wanted to hurt him, because he had gone through so much in life with his deformities. But once he made that field goal, the next time we had the opportunity we ignored his physical handicaps and treated him like anyone else. To this day that field goal is etched in every 1970 Detroit Lions player's mind because we actually thought it was going to be a fake field goal. We figured they'd try to go for a touchdown because there wasn't any way they were going to get a 63-yard field goal.

39

TERRIFIC TOES

LONG KICK LONG FORGOTTEN

Today people still marvel at 50-yard field goals. And Lions fans still talk about Tom Dempsey's record 63-yarder against them in New Orleans. But the talk of 1934 was the professional record field goal of 54 yards by Glenn Presnell of the Lions. The second-quarter kick was the only scoring as Detroit beat the Packers 3-0 at Bay Field in Green Bay on October 7. According to *The Detroit News* article on the game, the field goal could have been good from 64 yards away based on the height and direction.

As many great place-kickers as there have been in the NFL, few were better than Presnell. His 54-yarder was an NFL record that lasted 19 years and a Lions mark that stood for 61 years! And yet, he also was a star tailback, receiver, defensive back, and kickoff and punt returner. And, during his three years in Detroit, he also served as coach of the Lawrence Tech football team.

When Presnell died September 13, 2004, he was 99 and the league's second oldest living player. He was the only surviving member of the original Lions of 1934 and had played for the Ironton Tanks before joining the Portsmouth Spartans in 1931. He and his wife, Mary, were the Lions' special guests at the Pontiac Silverdome on October 9, 1994, when Detroit hosted the San Francisco 49ers. He was the game's honorary captain as the Lions celebrated their 60th anniversary and the league's 75th.

After his Lions career, Presnell coached football at Kansas and his alma mater, Nebraska, before serving three years in the Navy during World War II. He was the head coach at Eastern Kentucky from 1947-63 before becoming its athletic director until his retirement in 1974.

Tips from 'The Toe'

Jim Martin, who later was our special teams coach, was such a good kicker his last four years with the Lions that people hardly remember that the Notre Dame grad was a standout linebacker and offensive-defensive lineman with them from 1951 to 1961. It was almost by accident he started kicking, learning the skill in his rookie season of 1950 with the Cleveland Browns while waiting for kicking star Lou "The Toe" Groza, his friend, to get done with kicking drills at the end of practices.

In 1958 he was the Lions leading scorer with 49 points, on seven field goals and 28 point-after conversions. In 1959 he was the team MVP, and the following year he was back on top as leading scorer with 65 points (13 FGs and 26 PATs). His final season with the Lions was 1961, when he led the team again in scoring with 70 points (15 FGs, 25 PATs) and made the Pro Bowl team.

Despite all his high points that season, it was a bittersweet one. Two days after *The News' Sunday Pictorial* magazine color cover September 10 of Martin, he suffered a shoulder injury against the Bears. Yet he was back September 24 to kick three field goals to save the Lions' 16-15 triumph at Baltimore. But he was aching from more than a sore shoulder. A week earlier his eight-month-old son, Mitchell, died of leukemia—and that was the same day John Shallow, the father of his wife, Mandy, died of a heart attack. Martin retired in 1962, and Wayne Walker succeeded him as the Lions' place-kicker. Martin returned to the league to play at Baltimore in 1963 and Washington in 1964.

'Too quick'

The five-foot-eight, 160-pound soccer-style place-kicker Garo Yepremian seemed oblivious to his size as contrasted to the behemoths coming after the 22-year-old football novice from Cyprus. "They don't scare me. I'm too quick," he said, in a *Free Press* article October 14, 1966, by Jim Taylor. "They won't be able to find me. And the boys in front of me are pretty big. They'll protect me."

Yepremian didn't eat before a game and said it didn't have anything to do with being nervous, "It's just that my stomach gets filled up and I feel heavy inside. It's better for me to be empty."

Five weeks later Yepremian, who had never set foot on a football field before the season, kicked an NFL-record six field goals in a 32-31 triumph at Minnesota. "This week I tried wearing a football shoe on my right foot and a soccer shoe on my left," he told Whitey Sawyer of the AP. "The longer cleats on the football shoe stick in the ground and give me a better grip. I had been wearing soccer shoes on both feet, and I was slipping some." He led the team in scoring that season with 50 points.

Alex Karras hated Yepremian because he hated anyone little who drew attention to himself. If Garo missed a field goal, Alex would ride him to no end.

Terrific Toes

'THUNDERFOOT'

Herman Weaver was a country as corn. He had a great leg and probably was the second best punter I had seen at that time behind Ray Guy of Oakland. Coach Rick Forzano once told Weaver (1970-1976) he didn't care if his punts were short, as long as they were so high they couldn't be returned. When the Lions moved into the Silverdome (Pontiac Metropolitan Stadium) in 1975, Weaver had the benefit of no wind resistance—and a roof to aim at.

"I think he's punting now better than ever before," Forzano said late in the 1975 season, after a 17-10 Lions triumph over Minnesota in which Weaver blasted five punts for an average of 51 yards, including a 61-yarder.

"We told him to stop trying for distance," Forzano said, "just try to hit the roof. I don't care if he averages 29 yards, as long as they aren't returned."

Weaver's career best was 69 yards, and he is third on the team's all-time list for most punts, with 436. However, his 40.6 average is lowest among the top 10 (with Hall of Famer Yale Lary leading the way with a 44.3 average for his 503 punts).

In 1975, Weaver, nicknamed "Thunderfoot," led the National Football Conference with a 42-yard average, and that was second in the league to Guy. Weaver was drafted by Detroit in the ninth round from Tennessee, where he had 181 career punts without ever getting one blocked. Yet he never punted in high school. He started his college career as a wide receiver. In high school he was a star basketball player.

MANN WAS THE MAN

Kickers, it seems, are either heroes or goats. In football, there's no in between—or is there? My friend Errol Mann (1969-1976) was the man for eight seasons with the Lions as their place-kicker, often the one responsible for the victory—or the loss. Sometimes it was hard to determine whether he was being admired or admonished by Detroit fans.

Such was the case in a game December 6, 1970, in a 16-3 triumph at Tiger Stadium against the St. Louis Cardinals. Mann, who had scored 101 points the previous season, kicked three second-quarter field goals—and was roundly booed each time by the crowd of 56,363. Why? Because the fans were upset that coach Joe Schmidt was settling for field goals and not trying to get touchdowns.

Mann's field goals were from just 14, 13, and 10 yards out. The Lions had driven to the six-, eight-, and three-yard lines on those drives. "I always hear the booing and it used to bug me," Mann said after the game. "But now I just think about the field goal. But I still hear the fans booing. I know they know their football, and I can't knock them." The score was 9-3 until late in the final quarter when Mel Farr sprinted for a 28-yard touchdown, the game's only TD.

40

THEN AND NOW

So many things are so much different today than what they were in my playing days in the 1960s and 1970s—and certainly from what they must have been back in the mid-1930s when the Lions began as an NFL team. That includes everything from training facilities to pay.

WEIGHT ROOM

In my playing days we had a trainer, his assistant, and a small weight room, probably 20 feet by 20 feet. Today our weight room alone is probably 50 or 60 feet by 50 or 60 feet—with an upstairs and downstairs. Before we had trainer Kent Falb and his assistant. Today we have a trainer and multiple assistants, plus a strength and conditioning coach and his assistant.

At our old headquarters on Michigan Avenue we had a three-station universal gym. It had 350 pounds in free weights, a simple bench press and extension, a military press, two tables for taping, and a one-man whirlpool. As for the coaching staff, we had maybe six on the entire staff, and one of those was the head coach. Right now maybe there are 20 coaches and assistants. In the training room there may be five or six guys.

It's a business today. Back then it took you two weeks before training camp to start to get in shape. You really didn't get in shape until you got to camp. A great majority of guys had to work in the off-season because they didn't make enough money as players. Now, players don't have to work in the off-season, and many work out extensively and come into camp in good shape.

NEW OFFICES

The Lions offices were on Michigan Avenue and Eighth Street, a couple blocks from Tiger Stadium, when I joined the team. They had been there since 1949 when the facility was built specifically for them. The club signed a 10-year lease and had an option to purchase the building. When the team moved to Pontiac, it moved its offices there, too, and the Tigers bought the building because of a need for more office space.

When the Lions first came to Detroit their offices were in the Fisher Building, home of owner Dick Richards's WJR radio station. For many years their offices were in the Tuller Hotel (now empty).

SALARY CHANGES

In my rookie year I signed a $16,000 contract. My bonus was so small my agent wrote me a personal check to help me get by. You were living as a professional athlete and the downfall was getting caught up in that. You had to live like a professional and do things a professional would do, but you found out there just wasn't enough money. My first paycheck per week was about what they pay these guys today just to go in and lift weights for three days a week in the off-season so they can prolong their career.

Before moving to a new building on Michigan Avenue near Briggs Stadium, the Lions offices were here in the Tuller Hotel building.
Photo courtesy of the Detroit Lions

Amateurs Want a Shot

The Lions have conducted "Gong Shows" to check out the skills of ordinary athletes from the community. We got at least one player out of them, a fullback. In 2004, Jon Dykema, a summer intern in the public relations office, had better times in the skills competition at the tryouts than did the actual Lions.

Coach Potsy Clark, quoted in the August 19, 1934, *Detroit Times*, said many young men wanted to try out in training camp for the new team, guys who were "willing to pay their own expenses to come here…with the odds of 50 to 1 against them they won't survive the first week of practice…" Because of that, he said, "It's easy to see the prestige the National Football League has acquired during the past five years. Why, if we gave everybody who asks for a trial a chance between now and August 31, we would have 100 football players out at Cranbrook for our first practice session."

Portsmouth Era

When the Lions were the Portsmouth Spartans they played in a 12,000-seat stadium—but only about 3,000 would pay to show up to those Depression-era games on Sunday. On Fridays, however, 10,000 fans would turn out to watch a free scrimmage.

Portsmouth was on the Ohio River, some 90 miles south of Columbus on the Kentucky border. It had steel mills and a shoe factory all closed due to the Depression. Players dressed in a shed and hung their clothes on broom handles. A potbellied stove warmed the center of the room, and there was one lonely shower in the corner.

The 1929 Spartans were an independent pro team. In 1930 they joined the NFL and had a 4-6-3 record under Hal "Tubby" Griffen. Potsy Clark took over the next season and guided them to an 11-3 record, second behind the 12-2 Green Bay Packers. They were 6-2-4 in 1932 to finish third behind the 7-1-6 Bears and the 10-3-1 Packers. The franchise ended with a 6-5 record in 1933, second to the Bears.

G.A. Richards, who bought the team and moved it to Detroit, managed the Firestone Tire and Rubber Company in Akron, Ohio, in 1914 before moving to Detroit to start an auto dealership. It did very well, and he sold it to General Motors for $100,000 and became owner of one of America's pioneer radio stations, WJR in Detroit.

Ranch Reunion

In the summer of 1987, many of the former Lions from their great championship teams of the 1950s got together at a reunion in Frisco, Texas. Also there was Bob

Then and Now

These Portsmouth Spartans of 1929 were an independent team, joining the NFL the next season, then becoming the Detroit Lions in 1934.
Photo courtesy of the Detroit Lions

Reynolds, Lions radio play-by-play voice, who recounted the gathering in his August 1987 column in *Sports Fans' Journal*.

"They came together, at an imposing ranch outside Dallas, for two days and nights of fun and reminiscing dedicated to the first real 'leader of the pack'—Bobby Layne. There was a dinner, a rodeo later in the evening, and the next day an old-fashioned country and western barbeque and dance, all at the ranch. Each guest took home a video cassette of highlights of those great championship years—all this because the owner of the ranch never has forgotten his teammates and friends." The host was end Cloyce Box, owner of Box Ranch.

ALLITERATIVE ARRAY

At one point during the 1945 season, Lions coach Gus Dorais said he "found myself calling the names of three of our players in rapid succession: Radovich, Trebotich, and Uremovich. I got to thinking I had become a master of Russian." On their Lions player questionnaires, Bill Radovich, a 240-pound guard, and Emil Uremovich, a 240-pound tackle, listed themselves under nationality as "Americans," and 195-pound back Buzz Trebotich wrote "American of Scot-Check ancestry." Dorais added: "If we only had a Sinkwich, too." Star quarterback Frank Sinkwich was out for the season with an injury.

Farm Club Days

It may be hard to image the Lions as having farm clubs, but they did. One of them was the Wilkes-Barre, Pennsylvania, Indians, which Detroit played August 21, 1949, in an exhibition game. The Lions won 49-0 before 7,856 spectators. The Indians didn't get past their own 41-yard line. Three minutes into the game, Wally Triplett of the Lions scored a touchdown on a 61-yard run on a reverse to set the tone.

TOUGH GUYS

Don't Make Gramps Mad

I played with John Baker (DE, 1968) my rookie year. He was a defensive end who never smiled. He smoked a cigar and was a grandfatherly-type guy. He'd say very little, but one thing you wouldn't want to do was make him mad. It was fun to watch him against Roger Shoals in practices. Shoals wasn't going to get him mad, so Baker pretty much had his way. Big John could back it up. He had been in the league since 1958 and came to us from the Steelers. He established a reputation for almost killing quarterback Y.A. Tittle of the San Francisco 49ers with a tackle.

A Mean Smile

Offensive guard Chuck Walton (1967-1974) was tough. The first thing he'd do when you saw him was pull his two false teeth out and it made him look even tougher. He was a well-build, strong kid. He wasn't the greatest athlete in the world, but he was a fun-type guy. He had a lot of prankster in him. He always was laughing and creating a stir, especially against Alex Karras, because he had to play against him in practice every day.

Crushing Grip

Defensive back Bobby Williams (1969-1971), whose nickname was "Wild Child," was as strong as an ox. He could take a Coke bottle, wrap a towel around it, and crush it with his bare hands. His hands were the most powerful I've ever seen. He had a grip that would bring a big man to his knees.

'NUBS' WAS LIKE NAILS

Among the Lions' long list of hard-nosed linebackers was Charlie Weaver (1971-1981), who was from the University of Southern California. He was tough as nails and built without an ounce of fat on him. He had small hands, though, and we gave him the nickname of "Nubs." It seemed like he didn't have fingers, just all nubs. He was very strong and athletic. He could run, tackle, hit. The only thing he couldn't do was catch, because he had such small hands.

GETTING THE 'BREAKS'

When I played at Minnesota, we had a player, Aaron Brown, who broke his jaw and threw up. He just tightened his chin strap and kept playing. I don't recall any of my contemporaries with the Lions doing anything similar, but there's a story about one of the earlier Lions, Fred Vanzo, that deserves mention. The New York Giants drafted Vanzo (E, 1938-1941) out of Northwestern in 1938, but the Lions bought his contract in August and brought him to training camp. He was a tough player, to be sure. A year earlier in the Wildcats' game against Purdue he suffered a broken jaw and broken nose on successive plays—then, three minutes later, ran 68 yards for a touchdown to win the game.

"I had an old score to wipe out against Purdue when the game started," he told *The Detroit News*. "Two years before, as a sophomore fullback, I fumbled the ball on a buck over center, which cost us the game."

Vanzo also said in a game against Michigan he took a kickoff, ran down the field, and when two tacklers converged on him, instead of sidestepping or straight-arming them, he gave them a rolling block. "Force of habit overcame me," he said, and everyone in the stadium was amazed.

42

TRAINER TIPS

DIET REGIMENS

I was one of those guys who couldn't keep weight on. I had a recipe from my college days for a malt I'd drink every night, and I was able to put on 35 pounds "Training table" refers to the dining table where athletes have their meals together. At the Lions' training camp in 1940 at Cranbrook there actually were three training tables, as reported by John N. Sabo of the *Free Press*: There was the "fat men's table, the skinny guys' table, and the regulars' table."

Trainer Abe Kushner, Howie Weiss, and dietician Mrs. Elizabeth Bemis formed the tables. At the "fat" table sat tackles Bill Rogers (252 pounds), Steve Maronic (243), and Clem Crabtree (233); guards Bill Radovich (243) and Bill Feldhaus (243); plus center John Tsoutsovas (235). One of the players at the skinny table was Jack Morlock, a halfback from Marshall who came into camp at 167 pounds and gained eight in the first week, despite two-a-day practices. Crabtree, meanwhile, dropped to 223 pounds.

Kushner, talking of the fat men's table, said: "You should hear the big fellows cry for butter, cream, and sugar. But you can bet the crying doesn't do them any good."

GET A TAN

In June 1937, the *Detroit Times* ran an article listing Kushner's recommendations for off-season regimens. One was that players should work out in bare feet to toughen them. Also, Kushner said, "Get out under the sun. Every player will be expected to report with a good coat of tan over his body. Plenty of sunlight will prepare your body for a successful season. Swimming is not a good conditioning exercise. Don't overdo it.... 1. Start training by July 25. 2. Avoid bad habits. 3. Eat meals at regular hours. 4. Be sure to give yourself plenty of ankle and knee calisthenics."

43

TRAGEDIES

HUGHES'S SHOCKING DEMISE

There have been some scary moments at Lions games throughout their history, including a paralyzing injury to guard Mike Utley in 1991, but none was more devastating than the tragedy that took place October 24, 1971, at Tiger Stadium. That's when Detroit wide receiver Chuck Hughes (1970-1971), going back to the huddle in the final two minutes of a 28-23 upset loss to the Chicago Bears, collapsed and died.

The pass on that play was thrown to me and was incomplete, broken up by Dick Butkus. After I picked myself up off the ground I went back to the huddle and saw Chuck lying there. I told him to get up. We used to fake injuries in the last two minutes to stop the clock. All we knew was that he was lying there. Nobody was thinking death.

Reporters were on the phones calling in their game stories and few were aware of what was happening. Then doctors rushed onto the field. Phone receivers were dropped and binoculars picked up as reporters tried to see what was going on. Leads had to be changed abruptly, but all with uncertainty.

The Lions' two team physicians were there: Dr. Richard A. Thompson pounding Hughes's chest giving external heart massage, and Dr. Edwin Guise giving mouth-to-mouth resuscitation. Dr. Eugene Boyle, an anesthesiologist, even came out of the stands to help. But nothing could be done. Hughes never resumed breathing on his own.

Les Broad, a Lions fan who was at the game, was in the emergency room at Ford Hospital when Hughes's lifeless body was wheeled past him on a cart. Broad, who had suffered a reaction to a bee sting, collapsed and had to be revived on the same table where Hughes had been moments earlier.

"You're going to be OK," the doctor told him, Broad recalled in 2004. "We're not going to lose two in one day."

Tragedies

After the on-the-field death of Chuck Hughes in Detroit, the Lions and Packers stood for a moment of silence in Milwaukee in honor of the late wide receiver.
Photo courtesy of the Detroit Lions

An autopsy by Dr. Taisja Tworek, Wayne County Medical Examiner, revealed that the six-foot, 180-pound, 28-year-old Hughes died of a heart attack caused by a blood clot and hardening of the arteries. He was pronounced dead at Henry Ford Hospital less than an hour after the game.

Asked if the former Texas-El Paso star was playing football, unknowingly, with one foot in the grave, Guise said: "Essentially, that's true." Thompson said Hughes was given a cardiogram and that it, along with other laboratory tests, failed to show anything wrong. There was no method then to determine hardening of the arteries. "Obviously the circulation which he had to his heart was sufficient for him until he developed the clot," said Guise. "That apparently was the straw that broke the camel's back."

I was among the 70 Lions and team officials who flew by chartered jet to San Antonio, Texas, to attend the funeral. I remember his wife and son at the funeral. Hughes used to have this habit of stretching his hamstring muscles by sticking his leg out straight and pulling back on the shoelace. Every time I see someone do that now I think of Chuck.

Trio of Tragedies

In recent decades there were three tragedies that ended the brief careers of Lions who were developing into fine players. They are guards Eric Andolsek (1988-1991) and Mike Utley (1989-1991), and linebacker Reggie Brown (1996-1997).

We called Andolsek "Table," because his shoulders were so broad and chest so thick you could eat a seven-course meal on his shoulders. He was strong and powerful as a football player but soft-spoken and polite off the field.

He had developed into a Pro Bowl guard and was being counted on to anchor the offensive line the following year. But he was killed by the driver of a semi truck who had fallen asleep at the wheel traveling down a winding road and crashed into Eric as he worked in his yard in Louisiana.

Utley also was a big and strong guy. Though not the most gifted athlete, he outworked everyone at his position until he became a starter. He was improving every year, but his career ended in 1991 when he suffered a paralyzing injury. He gave a "thumbs-up" signal to his teammates and fans as he was carried off the field on a stretcher. That became an inspiration that helped Detroit finish first in the Central division of the NFC with a 12-4 record.

Utley continued to work on his recovery and developed some movement in his limbs. He has established the Mike Utley Foundation to support the further study of injuries such as his. He continues to be the symbol of courage throughout the NFL.

Brown was a tremendous athlete, another who was starting to emerge as a Pro Bowler. As he stepped in to fill a hole and make a tackle, he made the hit with his head downward, and it snapped vertebrae. At one point trainer Kent Falb said he stopped breathing. As many of his teammates later stood by his bedside, Reggie told them he would walk again. Several years later he returned to the Silverdome to walk on the same field where his tragedy had occurred in 1997.

Gone at 21

Lucien Reeberg might have been a teammate of mine had he not suffered a fatal heart attack—at age 21—after his rookie season of 1963. Few people today may have heard of the defensive lineman, but who knows how good he might have become? Reeberg, the team's 19th-round draft pick from Hampton Institute, died February 1, 1964, in Detroit Osteopathic Hospital while he was being prepared for surgical tests on his kidneys. The cause of death was listed as cardiac arrest due to uremic poisoning.

"I'm really shocked," Coach George Wilson said in Ben Dunn's story in *The News*, "the poor kid. I really felt he was going to be a great lineman. He had everything, size, talent, and desire." The six-foot-four, 290-pound Reeberg had signed a new contract two weeks earlier and was engaged to be married in June.

'OO' Killed in Crash

The biggest story of July 2, 1956, was the crash of a plane in the Grand Canyon that killed 128 people—including 13 from Detroit. Among those was Peter Whyte, a 15-year-old who was the Lions' water boy who used to wear number "00" on his back. His father, Detroit auto dealer Ray Whyte, owned a good share of Lions stock.

Torgy Passes the Reins

As a coach, Joe Schmidt was always one step ahead of us. I guess that's what made him such a great coach. He must have been one step ahead of everyone from the beginning, because he became the Lions' defensive signal caller as a rookie late in the 1953 season. But those duties came about as a result of a tragedy.

Coach Buddy Parker said Schmidt, the former University of Pittsburgh star, would replace LaVern Torgeson for the December 6 game at home against the Bears. Torgeson's wife, Mary Lou, had just died at the hospital of a liver ailment. She was just 24.

The team was very solemn after hearing the news at a Wednesday practice that Mrs. Torgeson had lapsed into a coma. Parker, whose father had died just three weeks earlier, dismissed practice early. "This is a close-knit squad, and Mary Lou's death was shocking," he said later. Torgeson said he wanted to come back the next week for the last regular-season game, December 13, at the New York Giants.

Parker said Schmidt "has learned a lot this season. I'm sure he'll handle Torgy's job." *Free Press* writer Bob Latshaw said Schmidt "had all the mechanical attributes needed by a pro linebacker. He's big [6-0, 220], rugged and fast. He covers well on pass defense and is fast enough to help out on tackles virtually everywhere on the field."

Freak Accident

Doak Walker was a superstar for the Lions almost from the day he joined the team in 1950, but things looked bleak for a short time in June of 1952 when Walker, who volunteered to help out at the U.S. Open Golf Tournament at Northwood Country Club in the Dallas area, smashed his elbow through a car window while trying to push the car from the front of his own car. The result was a severed triceps muscle of his right arm above the elbow. He recovered quickly from the freak accident, and it didn't hamper his career.

Early End

Wayne Clark, a 36-year-old former Lions end who played for Detroit in 1944-45, was presumed drowned in heavy surf at Redondo Beach, California, where he had been fishing off a pier with a 16-year-old boy early in 1955. The AP story said he told the boy he was a good swimmer and jumped in to show him. When he didn't come up, the boy went for help. Lifeguards and helicopter search parties couldn't find Clark, whose wife, Christine, had been sleeping in the car while her husband fished.

44

TRAVEL TRAVAILS

MY FEAR OF FLYING

Aerodynamics doesn't make sense to me. How could anything as heavy as an airplane fly? I definitely was afraid of flying, so to deal with it I'd try to fall asleep before takeoff and be asleep on the landing. It was the fear of taking off and landing, with someone else controlling a huge piece of machinery that bothered me. It got to the point where I didn't care and just said to myself, "If I die, I die."

The first time I flew on a plane was when I went to the University of Minnesota on my recruiting visit. It was the first time I had ever been out of North Carolina. Of course, in college we flew to our games, but it wasn't like taking trips to the West Coast. We mostly were going on short trips to Big Ten cities. With the Lions, my worst plane trip came when we flew to Texas for the funeral of Chuck Hughes, who died tragically of a heart attack after collapsing on the field near the end of a game at Tiger Stadium. On the way back from the funeral, the plane blew an engine, and we had to make an emergency landing in Dallas.

There was another time I particularly remember. It came after we won a game following a long losing streak. The plane was bouncing around in a thunderstorm, with lightning. I actually believed that the plane got hit by lightning. There was a huge drop and the pilot came on the loudspeaker and said it was God's way of applauding our first victory. We had a 14-game schedule at the time and I said, "Hell, 1-13 won't be bad. If this is what we have to go through, I'd rather take the loss."

GREEN-GILLED LIONS

Airplanes in 1950 could be bounced around by the elements a lot easier than what players a couple decades later would learn to expect. The Lions' charter flight

August 19, 1950, was a particularly rough one. The team was flying to Pittsburgh for a preseason game and all 52 players got airsick after the plane bounced around in a violent rain and electrical storm. All of them were "green around the gills," *The News* reported.

V.P. Killed

Frank Pierce, 49-year-old president of Dearborn Motors Corp. and the second vice president of the Lions, didn't get a chance to see the team blossom as a super franchise in the 1950s. He was killed shortly before the team emerged as champions when the private plane that was taking off from the airport in Charlotte, North Carolina, crashed. Pierce, a former General Motors vice president, suffered a head injury. His wife, Christine, and four others were injured.

45

TV TALES

Usually our collective bargaining agreement when I was a player was tied into whatever the NFL's TV deal was, although the union wasn't as strong as it is today and players didn't have much power. One or two player representatives would meet with the league and it was the beginning of the development that included the power TV had in the NFL.

It's a shame that a lot of the old-timers in the game, who lived and died for it, weren't able to experience the benefits that the newer generation of players have experienced because of the enormous revenues generated by television.

GREAT TIMING

William Clay Ford hit the jackpot when he purchased the Lions in 1964 for $4.5 million. The team soon signed a lucrative TV contract with CBS that would have been unheard of a couple years earlier—and which was for more than twice the amount newspapers speculated.

"Oh how those 144 former Lions stockholders must be moaning," wrote George Puscas in the January 25, 1964, *Free Press*, after CBS agreed to pay the league $28.2 million over two seasons through 1965. Each team would get $1 million-plus both years. The Lions payroll was $600,000 and total operations ran $1.5 million a year. Profits in 1962 exceeded $500,000, the *Free Press* reported. Losing bids came from ABC ($26.1 million) and NBC ($21.5 million).

NOT PEANUTS THEN

It was huge money then, but by today's multimillion-dollar television contract standards, the NFL TV deal in 1962 would seem like peanuts. It paid $320,000 to each team.

Oops, We're Sorry

In November 1960, WJBK-TV, Channel 2 in Detroit ran a large newspaper ad apologizing to viewers who missed a touchdown that was scored while a commercial was running. "Had we been able to ascertain that the timeout had been cut short and play resumed, the game would have been rejoined immediately," the station declared, adding that the game was its first priority.

Only Two TV Games

Lions fans have it made today, being able to watch their team on TV virtually every game. There isn't much worry any more about local blackouts on home games, because at Ford Field there are far fewer seats than at the massive Silverdome, so games are more apt to be sold out, thus allowing for local TV showings.

One of the first official functions held at the new Lions offices at Michigan and Eighth Street was a board meeting August 15, 1949, to discuss that new-fangled box called a television. Though few families had TVs, the Lions did televise games in 1948. But they announced after their 1949 meeting that "television is out for the Detroit Lions." According to one director, only two games, under league supervision, would be shown. TV, of course, would grow immensely and help assure profitable seasons for NFL owners.

Old Sponsor Quits

Goebel Beer, which had sponsored Lions games on radio and TV for 14 years, quit doing that in May 1960. It had shared sponsorship the previous season with Speedway gas and Marlboro cigarettes. Lions president Edwin Anderson used to be Goebel president.

New Cash Cow

As the NFL progressed into the 1950s, the new cash cow of television suddenly was making things easier for team owners. *The News* reported in May 1953 that the league's TV deal with Westinghouse to televise 14 games would net $1.347 million. The *Philadelphia Bulletin*, though, said the deal was for 19 games and that each team would get $50,000. The Lions also worked out a contract to televise five of its away games in the Detroit area.

With that money, though, came the inevitable TV control, as indicated by this May 17, 1953, *Free Press* headline: "TV Forces Lions to Shift Two Games."

Big Antennas

In the 1950s when there was no local TV for home games, people often relied on big roof antennas in hopes of picking up the signal from the stations in Flint (WJRT) or Lansing (WJIM). The antennas cost $7-$20 installed.

The AP reported in January 1959 that the Lions suffered no ill effects from such efforts the previous season and would continue to black out games within a 75-mile radius. Of the 74 bars that advertised "See all games here," 57 were tuned to the game, and less than half had a good picture, according to the report. Two bars had special equipment, costing $105, to pick up the signal.

A *Free Press* story said the Lindell bar's business was up 40 percent one particular Sunday because of the away game being televised there, and the owner of the Willis Show Bar said his business was up. Even the Snowden Dairy said it had increased business on football Sundays because it installed a special antenna, something the North Hills Country Club near Birmingham also had done.

46

WEATHER ADVENTURES

Bad Weather Games

I remember one year when the Minnesota Vikings visited Tiger Stadium for the Thanksgiving Day game, there was a snowstorm. You couldn't see the game. And I recall a mudfest when we played the Philadelphia Eagles. And we played the Green Bay Packers away in a downpour. Even motorcycle police escorting us to the stadium got stuck. Those are my recollections, but they of course weren't anything new.

Arctic Green Bay

Another year when we played in Green Bay it probably was the second or third coldest game ever there. Mickey Zofko was our kickoff return guy. He received a ball on a kickoff and ran 30 or 40 yards and was probably running for a touchdown before he realized it was so cold that he had dropped the ball on about the five-yard line.

We had a defensive end who broke his thumb in the game. He didn't realize it until Tuesday when his hands finally thawed out. That also was the same game in which Mel Farr was standing on a heater and had his cape up over him, not realizing there was smoke coming up out of the top of the hood. Everyone looked down and his shoes were burning.

Scoreless in Deluge

No telling what went through new Lions owner Fred Mandel's mind as his team opened its season September 16, 1940, in a most unusual way: against the Chicago Cardinals in Buffalo, New York, in a deluge, at night, with the outcome being a scoreless tie. The lights even went out at halftime.

The game was at Civic Stadium, played before 18,048 spectators who had to brave thunder, lightning, and pouring rain. There were 12 fumbles and even a bad snap by superstar center Alex Wojciechowicz. The rain started 40 minutes before game time and lasted two and a half hours. Detroit had just five first downs and the Cardinals two.

Coach Jimmy Conzelman of the Cards decided to have his team punt on first down every time they had the ball in the second half in hopes of getting a loose ball. Chicago didn't try a single running play in the second half, except on a bad snap on punt formation.

DITCHED

Jim McDonald (B, 1938-1939), whose duties as a blocking halfback in 1938 were changed to that of a running back in 1939, had a rather harrowing experience of the winter between seasons. It seems he was driving 85 miles an hour when his car went off the highway and into a 10-foot ditch, turning over two and a half times.

"My father came out and looked at the heap of junk that remained," the former Ohio State player told *The News*. "Finally, he shook his head and said to me, 'Son, either you live right or were born lucky, and I think it's the latter.'"

Celebrate the Variety of Michigan and American Sports in These Other New Releases from Sports Publishing!

Michigan: Where Have You Gone?
by Jim Cnockaert

- 6 x 9 hardcover
- 250 pages
- photos throughout
- $19.95 (2004 release)

Riding with the Blue Moth
by Bill Hancock

- 6 x 9 hardcover
- 256 pages
- photos throughout
- $24.95

Tales from Michigan Stadium: Volume II
by Jim Brandstatter

- 5.5 x 8.25 hardcover
- 200 pages
- photos throughout
- $19.95 (2005 release)

Mike Ditka: Reflections on the 1985 Bears
by Mike Ditka with Rick Telander

- 5.5 x 8.25 hardcover
- 200 pages
- photos throughout
- $19.95

Tales from Michigan Stadium (softcover)
by Jim Brandstatter

- 5.5 x 8.25 softcover
- 200 pages
- photos throughout
- $14.95 (2005 release)

The Holyfield Way: What I Learned from Evander
by Jim Thomas with commentary by Evander Holyfield

- 6 x 9 hardcover • 256 pages
- eight-page photo insert
- $24.95

Detroit Pistons: Champions at Work
by The Detroit News

- 8.5 x 11 hard/softcover
- 128 pages • color photos
- $19.95 (hardcover)
- $14.95 (trade paper)

Dick Enberg: Oh My!
by Dick Enberg with Jim Perry

- 6 x 9 hardcover • 256 pages
- 16-page color-photo section
- $24.95
- Bonus "Beyond the Book" DVD included!

Tales of the Magical Spartans
by Tim Staudt and Fred Stabley Jr.

- 5.5 x 8.25 hardcover
- 200 pages
- photos throughout
- $19.95 (2003 release)

Ferdie Pacheco: Blood in My Coffee
by Ferdie Pacheco

- 6 x 9 hardcover
- 256 pages
- photo insert
- $24.95

All books are available in bookstores everywhere!
Order 24-hours-a-day by calling toll-free **1-877-424-BOOK (2665)**.
Also order online at **www.SportsPublishingLLC.com**.